EXPLORING ENOCHIAN WORLDS

For CJC and KH
with love

EXPLORING ENOCHIAN WORLDS

VISIONARY JOURNEYS THROUGH
THE ANGELIC UNIVERSE

of Dr. John Dee and Edward Kelley

Robin E. Cousins

Thoth Publications

This edition published by Thoth Publications 2021

© Robin Cousins 2020

Robin Cousins asserts the moral right to be identified as the author of this work.

A CIP catalogue record for this book is available from the British Library

All rights reserved. No part of this publication may be reproduced, stored in a retrieval system, or transmitted, in any form or by any means, electronic, mechanical, photocopying, recording or otherwise, without the prior permission of the publishers.

Cover and text design by Helen Surman

Published by
Thoth Publications
64 Leopold Street, Loughborough, LE11 5DN

ISBN 9781870450911

Web address: www.thoth.co.uk

email: enquiries@thoth.co.uk

CONTENTS

Acknowledgments 7
List of Illustrations 8
Introduction 9

Section One: THE ENOCHIAN UNIVERSE

1. The Quest of Doctor Dee 16
2. The Angelic Universe of John Dee and Edward Kelley 21
   The Forty-Eight Angelic Keys or Calls
   The Thirty Aires or Æthyrs
   The Great Table of Earth
   The Physical World in detail
3. Invocations and the *Call of the Thirty Æthyrs* 32
   A Book of Supplications and Invocations
   Claves Angelicæ – the Angelic Keys
4. The Call of the Thirty Æthyrs in English, Angelic and 39
   Phonetic Angelic
5. Guide to the Operation 45
   Creating a Sacred Space
   Lesser Banishing Ritual of the Pentagram
   The Ritual
   Closing Ceremony
   A Note on Enochian Sex Magick
   Magical Health and Safety
6. The Æthyrs, Qabalah and Correspondences 63

Part Two: AN ENOCHIAN TRAVELOGUE

Preamble 71
7. The Elemental Worlds of the Four Quarters 72
8. The Aires from the Thirtieth (TEX) to the Twenty-First (ASP) 77
9. The Aires from the Twentieth (CHR) to the Eleventh (ICH) 90
10. The Aires from the Tenth (ZAX) to the First (LIL) 100
11. Elements of the Watchtowers and TEX the Thirtieth Æthyr 112
    – a group working

Section 1: The Ritual 113
Section 2: The Visions 128

CONTENTS

Part Three: APPENDICES — 143

I Aleister Crowley and Enochian Magic — 144
II Aleister Crowley, Victor Neuberg and the Æthyrs: The Itinerary — 161
III The Angelic or Enochian Language — 167
IV *The Qabalistical Invocation of Solomon* — 171
V The Latin wall inscription in Tadeáš Hájek's study — 175
VI A Kelley Miscellany — 177
VII Enochian Visions - A form for recording results — 182

Select Bibliography — 186

ACKNOWLEDGMENTS

Negotiating the Enochian Universe of John Dee and Edward Kelley has proved to be a long journey and I should like to thank all my fellow travellers – Bali Beskin, Luke Bond, Melissa Harrington, Elaine Knight, Dave Marsh, Stephen Schofield and James Tuckett – who accompanied me at various times across the Great Table of Earth and through the Æthyrs.

A big thank you goes to Geraldine and Bali Beskin of the Atlantis Bookshop and Elaine Knight for allowing their premises to become temporary Enochian temples and for supplying welcome refreshments to the weary astral adventurers.

I am also most grateful to Barbara Prichard and the late Christopher Upton for their translations of various Latin passages.

Many of the illustrations and diagrams have been specifically created or photographed for this work. All sources are gratefully acknowledged. Some items are in the public domain and if this was indeterminable, every reasonable effort has been made to locate the copyright holders.

Finally, I wish to give special thanks to Carol C. and Keith Howes for their endless patience, periodic proof-reading, support and advice, not to mention their many helpful suggestions regarding the text and illustrative material. This book is for them.

LIST OF ILLUSTRATIONS

1. Establissement de la Fontaine- Chaude [Hammam Salihine], c.1912.   12
2. Dee's *Sigillum Dei Æmaeth* in the British Museum.   17
3. A rough sketch of Dee's House at Mortlake.   18
4. The Thirty Aires or Æthyrs.   22
5. Edward Kelley's *Vision of the Four Castles*.   26
6. The Great Table of Earth.   27
7. The Eastern Watchtower.   28
8. The Fourth Sub-Angle of the Eastern Watchtower.   30
9. Hájek's House, 1870.   46
10. Antonín Levý. *Betlémské Náměstí*. 1869 (detail).   47
11. Kelley's Tower, Prague.   49
12. The Elemental Signs.   54
13. Qabalistic Tree of Life.   67
14. Sketch of the casket made during the meditation.   80
15. Sign of DES, the Twenty-Sixth Æthyr.   81
16. The Four Seals of the Watchtowers   107
17. Gustave Doré. *Empyrean*, from Dante's *Divina Commedia: Paradiso*.   142
18. Kelley and Paul Waring at Walton-Le-Dale.   148
19. Třeboň medieval fortications.   149
20. The Black Cross rearranged as the Tablet of Union.   150
21. L'Arba – Arrival of the train from Algiers, c.1909.   156
22. Aumale (Sour El Ghozlane), Bou Saâda Gate (La Porte Sud), c.1910.   157
23. Biskra - The Royal Hotel, January 1910.   158
24. General view of Bou Saâda, c. 1920.   162
25. Tolga, before 1907.   164
26. Hammam Salihine, c. 1900.   165
27. Map of Crowley and Neuberg's Algerian Odyssey.   166
28. St Leonard's Church, Walton-le-Dale.   181

INTRODUCTION

There are few published accounts of Angelic or Enochian magical pathworkings. The most well known are accounts of visionary journeys resulting from scrying the Thirty Aires or Æthyrs (as Aleister Crowley called them) which surround the physical world or planet Earth like the skins of an onion. In this work, the terms are used interchangeably. In Krakow, on 21st May 1584, the Angel Nalvage described the Aires to Edward Kelley (1555-97):

"Understand, therefore, that from the fire to the earth, there are 30 places or abidings: one above and beneath another."[1]

Two important accounts of these travels are the pioneering original by Aleister Crowley, the notorious *The Vision and the Voice* or *Liber 418* (1972 and 1998) and recently *The Winds of Wisdom* (2017) by Thelemite scholar and practitioner David Shoemaker. Understandably, both records are heavily influenced by Thelema, which is reflected in both the nature of the visions and in the occasional interpretive commentaries.

This current work records visionary journeys in John Dee and Edward Kelley's Great Table of Earth, which details the angelic structure of the physical world, and in the surrounding Thirty Aires of the celestial world. Further details regarding the Great Table are found in Chapter Two below. The scrying was undertaken over more than twenty years. It began as a group working, but was completed by the present author after the group disbanded soon after working DES, the Twenty-Sixth Æthyr.

The work departs from the Thelemic tradition and Enochian procedures stemming from the Hermetic Order of the Golden Dawn and the work of Aleister Crowley by returning to the original angelic system of Dee and Kelley. It opens the door to the exploration of the four classical elements of the terrestrial world and their attendant angels, which are all detailed on the Great Table. This in turn provides a firm spiritual basis from which to commence the journey.

The original version of the Great Table of Earth was received in Krakow during May and June, 1584. Dee subsequently wrote the *Book of Supplications and Invocations*

---

1. John Dee. *A true and faithful relation of what passed for many years between Dr John Dee ... and some spirits*, ed. Meric Casaubon [Hereafter *T&FR*] (London:1659), p.140.

for the angels of the Great Table. Three years later, a revised version of the Table was delivered to Kelley by the angel Raphael that reordered the internal structure and changed some of the angelic names, thereby invalidating Dee's invocations. A new set do not appear to have been written. Kelley may have had ulterior motives and the divine origin of the Table of Raphael has been questioned.

The Table of Raphael was adopted by the Golden Dawn and Crowley for their Enochian studies and various so-called improvements were made, making the system even more complicated. Originally, the four quarters of the Great Table were purely directional. Under the Golden Dawn system, they became elemental: the Eastern Quarter becoming the Air Tablet; the Southern quarter now the Fire Tablet, and so on. All rather unnecessary, considering that each quarter of the original table has their own angels for the *Knowledge and Understanding of the Four Elements*. For further information on the differences between the two systems, see Appendix I, a revised transcript of this author's talk, A*leister Crowley and Enochian Magic*, for the Aleister Crowley Conference held at Clun, Shropshire, in 2014.[2]

Despite the validity of the Table of Raphael being in doubt, it cannot be denied that, owing to its constant use by the Golden Dawn, Crowley and all their followers for over a 100 years, the revised system, now known as Neo-Enochiana, has become imbued with a spiritual power of its own, no less effective. Ultimately, therefore, it is a matter of personal choice which system is employed.

The following record is Dee-purist, i.e., based on the original system as received in Krakow. The work is a system for one's own spiritual and personal development. It takes place outside of physical reality in the spirit vision or the mind's eye, sometimes projected into a crystal, magic mirror or other device, if the operator is fortunate enough to possess such talent.

As mentioned, the spirit travels commence with the exploration of the four elements of each of the four quarters of the terrestrial world of the Great Table, in order to provide a strong spiritual foundation from which to explore the celestial realms of the Aires, leading to the threshold of the super celestial worlds of the angels, archangels and the world of the Holy Spirit beyond.

Neither Crowley nor David Shoemaker utilised this approach. Crowley, in fact, actually began working with the Great Table of the Watchtowers after his work on the Æthyrs, but it was a disaster and he gave up. Here is his account:

---

[2] The conference was organised by the Pagan Federation Mid Wales and West.

"The rites being over and their lesson learnt, I felt free to go back to my beloved Sahara. As before, I took [Victor] Neuburg with me and motored down from Algiers to Bou Saâda. ... It was part of the programme to obtain visions of the sixteen sub-elements, as a sort of pendant to the Æthyrs, but the time was not yet. We began, but the results were so unsatisfactory that we broke off." [3]

By scrying the Æthyrs first, it meant he was actually working the system back to front. Each quarter has four angels responsible for the elements in that quarter. It is to them that the seeker must first appeal in order to set the whole process in motion.

One should not expect instant results. Changes will take place gradually with realisations occurring over a period of time. The whole exercise could take a number of years. Certain Aires create a "ring-pass-not" situation and progress halts until the block or the problem is faced, acknowledged, and accepted by the practitioner. As David Shoemaker writes in *The Winds of Wisdom*:

"Sometimes this may be a simple as nodding one's head inwardly at the truth revealed in a vision, and moving on to the next Æthyr the very next day. At other times, it may require many months of analysis and meditation, or even sweeping changes in one's external life, to fully integrate the vision and move on." (page v.)

Crowley comments on his own difficulties as follows:

"Two or three times I had found it difficult to get into the Æthyr [the 18th]; there were bars which I understood as not to be passed by the profane. The progressive sublimity and solemnity made me tremble lest I should not be worthy to behold the mysteries that lay in the future." [4]

And referring to himself in *Magick in Theory and Practice*, he writes:

"His chief difficulty was that sometimes He was at first unable to pierce their veils. In fact, as the Book [i.e., The Vision and the Voice] shows, it was only by virtue of successive and most exalted initiations undergone in the Æthyrs themselves that He was able to penetrate beyond the 15th. The Guardians of such fortresses know how to guard." [5]

---

3. *The Confessions of Aleister Crowley*, ed. John Symonds and Kenneth Grant [Hereafter *The Confessions*] (New York: Bantam Books, 1971), p.708.
4. *The Confessions*, p.673.

It took Crowley three days to complete his scrying of ARN, the Second Æthyr, during his Algerian odyssey. He commenced it on the morning of 18 December 1909 at the Royal Hotel, Biskra, where he was staying.

"The work had to be broken off and the Invocation repeated. Yet again I found the strain insupportable, and had to break off, and go to the hot baths of Hammam Salahin[6] and I continued, immersed to the neck in the hot sulphur spring. The water somehow soothed my nerves, enabling me to experience the Æthyr without physical collapse. Even so, I could not get to the end and only did so after over more than two days' concentrated consecration of myself."[7]

1. N.D. Photo.[8] *Environs de Biskra. Establissement de la Fontaine-Chaude* [Hammam Salihine]. Postcard c.1912 (Author's collection)

The experience at Hammam Salihine proved draining and Crowley sank back exhausted. Victor Neuberg, *"fearing that he might be drowned assisted him to come out of the pool"*.[9]

David Shoemaker scryed the Thirty Æthyrs between 2007 and 2011, while it took Crowley nine years, beginning in Mexico in 1900 with the Thirtieth and Twenty-Ninth Æthyrs. The remaining twenty-eight were completed in Algeria, after a long hiatus, at the end of 1909.

The present scrying is much more involved, beginning as a group of four working the elements of the quarters and the Thirtieth Aire, TEX, in October 1995.

5. Crowley. *Magick in theory and practice* (New York: Castle Books,[1960]), p.152.
6. Hammam Salihine is a thermal spa about 7 km from Biskra. It is an ancient Roman bath founded during the reign of Vespasian (69 -79 AD)
7. *The Confessions*, p.678-679.

INTRODUCTION

The group disbanded after the Twenty-Sixth Aire in Spring 1996 and I continued alone until August 1999, ceasing after the Seventh Aire, DEO, for a variety of reasons. In September 2008, a group of six explored the elemental worlds and the Thirtieth Æthyr once more. The working was an adjunct to an Enochian Magic course run by the author at the Atlantis Bookshop, London. The results of this session are included in the present volume, along with the ritual and a copy of the form used for recording the participants' experiences. The remaining six Aires were completed during 2018.

Before proceeding to the record of the travels, a description of the structure of the Angelic or Enochian universe follows. It is not an in-depth study, but the information should be sufficient to provide a basic understanding of the system. The methods employed to scry the Thirty Aires or Æthyrs and the Great Table of the Watchtowers, along with the associated rituals, are also offered as a possible way to gain access to the Enochian worlds.

Robin E. Cousins
Norwich, England, 2021.

---

8. Photographer brothers Etienne and Louis-Antonin Nuerdein. From 1875, the Nuerdein Frères began publishing postcards. Later, their work was funded by the French government to promote colonial tourism in Algeria.
9. Crowley, *The Vision and the Voice* (1972), p. 241, n.63.

PART ONE

THE ENOCHIAN UNIVERSE

CHAPTER ONE

THE QUEST OF DOCTOR DEE

John Dee (1527-1609) had long sought the mysteries of creation. By the late 1570s he had given up trying to discover the Secrets of the Universe by normal means, believing spiritual secrets could only be learnt from god via the angels. He later explained this to the Emperor Rudolf II in Prague on 3 September 1584.

"... all my lifetime I have spent in learning ... to come by the best knowledge that man might attain unto in the world: And I found (at length) that neither any man living, nor any Book I could yet meet withal, was able to teach me those truths I desired, and longed for."

He decided, therefore,

"to make intercession and prayer to the giver of wisdom and all good things, to send me such wisdom, as I might know the nature of his creatures; and also the means to use them to his honour and glory." [10]

It was not a new concept. The Neo-Platonist philosopher Iamblichus (c. AD 245 - 327) had said.

"A god, an angel, and a good daemon instruct man in what their proper essence consists ... Angels and daemons always receive truth from the gods, so they never assert anything contrary to this." Iamblichus, *De mysteriis*, Venice 1497.

From about 1579 Dee started regular scrying sessions at his home in Mortlake

---

10. *T&FR*, p.231.

attempting to contact angels. He had little success with his original scryers Bartholomew Hickman and Barnabus Saul. However, everything changed with arrival of Edward Kelley, who it transpired was an experienced alchemist, magician and scryer. He was just the person Dee required. On Thursday 8 March 1582, Kelley accompanied a Mr Clerkson on a visit to Dee. He was introduced as Edward Talbot, which later proved to be an alias, allegedly used to conceal a dubious past. This was rumoured to include necromancy and being pilloried in Lancaster for forging wills, for which his ears were supposedly cropped.[11] On Saturday 10 March 1582, Kelley arrived alone *"willing and desyrous to see or shew something in spirituall practise"*.

Dee *"confesed myself, long tyme to haue byn desyrous to haue help in my philosophicall studies throwgh the Cumpany and information of the blessed Angels of God."*[12] He was sufficiently impressed and immediately brought forth "my stone in the frame". Kelley immediately transformed Dee's tentative magical tinkerings and via his mediumship the system of Angelic or Enochian magic practised today started to develop. Dee, a self-confessed hopeless scryer, meticulously set-down all the information, tabulating and ordering it into a workable system. Dee's dog-

2. Dee's "Sigillum Dei Æmaeth" in the British Museum (Photograph © R.E. Cousins)

11. For further information on Kelley's ears, see Appendix VI.
12. Peterson, Joseph, ed. *John Dee's Five Books of Mysteries*. (San Francisco: Weiser Books, 2003), p. 66.

with-a-bone mentality ensured that anything he was not crystal-clear about, he had Kelley and/or the angels clarify until patience was tested. Dee's magical operations received a complete makeover.

By end of the day of Kelley's arrival, details of the Holy Table of Practice had been received. This was the beginning of the Angelic System of Magic. By the end of month, they had details of the *Sigillum Dei Æmaeth* (Seal of God and Truth), which was placed under the crystal on the Holy Table. Filled with holy names, it was a mandala or talisman of wax designed to attract divine forces to the place of working. It was also used for protection against evil. Smaller versions were placed under each table-leg. Such seals had various forms and were popular in Medieval magic. The angels told Dee his version was perfect.

One of the earliest versions is found in the thirteenth century grimoire or magical manual, *Liber Juratis* or *The Sworn Book*, for obtaining visions of the "true and living" God. It was consecrated as follows:

> "First, the worker must be clean, not impure, and should do so with devotion, not cunningly. He must not eat or drink until the work is completed, and the blood, with which the writing will be done, must first be blessed, as will be declared afterward. Then the seal should be suffumigated with amber, musk, aloes, labdanum - white and red [a resinous gum from rock rose], mastick, olibanum margarith [Frankincense pearls or tears], and [Frank]incense, calling upon and praying to the Lord, as will be taught afterwards concerning the divine vision."[13]

3. "A rough sketch of Dee's House at Mortlake", possibly early 19th century.[14]

---

13 Peterson, Joseph, *The Sworn Book Of Honorius* (Lake Worth, FL:Lake Worth, Ibis Press, 2016), p.75.

By November 1582, they had developed a system of planetary magic known as *De Heptarchia Mystica* (The Mystic Sevenfold Kingdom). Each day has a King, Prince and 42 Ministers with special functions

Soon the House in Mortlake was overrun by *"spiritual creatures"*. On March 15th a *"great company of wicked spirits"* appeared, amongst which *"one most horrible and grisly there hung and approaching to our heads; and scorning and gnashing at us"*. Luckily, a few days later on March 20th Kelley saw *"an innumerable multitude of Angels in the Chamber or study abowt us, very beautiful with wynges of fyre"*, which would protect them from the wicked.[15]

Just over a year later on 26 March 1583, the basic form of the so-called Angelic or Enochian Alphabet was delivered to Kelley. It was supposedly the alphabet of the speech of God and the angels, the speech of Adam, the perfect language. There are strong arguments for and against it being genuine language. To Dee and Kelley this seemed the beginning of the revelation from God of the Secrets of Creation. The ability to converse with God like Adam had been lost, together with the Holy Language, with Adam's expulsion from Paradise. The Celestial Speech had to be rediscovered "to teach me those truths I desired, and longed for", said Dee. The Bible legend relates that Enoch was the only descendant of Adam not to die and was the last man to learn the Divine Language and write down the secrets in a Book, later lost in the Flood.

Genesis 5: 24. *And Enoch walked with God: and he was not: for God took him.*

For Dee this proved reunion with the divine from an earthly existence was possible. According to the angels, Dee and Kelley were apparently the first individuals since Enoch privileged to learn the Angelic tongue. However, it was not the first time that a claim for the discovery of the HolyLanguage had been made. At that time, the existence of the Divine Language was generally accepted. In 1530 the Venetian Priest, Joannes Augustinus Pantheus, published the alchemical work, known as *Vorarchadumia*, which contained an "Alphabet of Enoch". Dee had a copy that he annotated and which is now in the British Library. The sixteenth century Central European grimoire *Libellus Verenen Nigro Sacer* aka the *Tuba Veneris* or *Trumpet*

---

14. From Hippocrates Junior [Major J.Waller], *The Predicted Plague* (London, 1900).Unauthenticated, the sketch was from the collection of antiquary William Upcott (1779-1845) which was sold by Sotheby after his death. Dee's house was described by Sir Richard Phillips in *A morning's walk from London to Kew* (London, 1817). The house was demolished during the nineteenth century.

15. Peterson, Joseph, ed. *John Dee's Five Books of Mysteries*, p. 82 and 124.

of Venus (c.1580), incorrectly attributed to John Dee, states: *"Whereby, if anything be imparted to an evil spirit by a good one, he calls and orders by the appropriate summons, though this may be in a language unintelligible to us mortals"*.[16] For more information on the Angelic or Enochian Language, including the alphabet, please see Appendix III.

During 1583, Dee and Kelley received a mysterious angelically transmitted book, known as the *Liber Loagaeth* aka *Book of the Speech from God*, that was apparently the lost *Book of Enoch* itself.

On 5 May 1583, the Angel Uriel said of the Book:

"This boke and holy key, which unlocketh the Secrets of God – his determination, as concerning the beginning, present being, and end of this world, is so reverent and holy."[17]

It is too complex to believe it was an invention of Kelley's. It includes forty-eight tables of alphabetical squares. They cover both sides of each leaf of the book, making a total of 96 actual grids of 49 x 49 little squares of letters resulting in 2401 squares per side. The book also contains a series of invocations in the Angelic Language that have proved impossible to translate.

Later the *Liber Loagaeth* was used to generate a series of invocations known as the Angelic Keys or Calls from which the knowledge of Angelic language comes as a result of translations being provided. The Angelic language of the *Liber Loagaeth* is completely different from that of the Calls and has remained incomprehensible. The Angelic system continued to develop in Poland in 1584. In Krakow, they received the basic information detailing the structure of the Angelic or Enochian universe.

---

16. Warburg Insitute, London. MS FBH 510, p.4-5. See also R.E. Cousins, *Dr Dee and the Dark Venus*, 2nd ed. (London: Neptune Press, 2013), p131.
17. Peterson, ibid. p. 395.

CHAPTER TWO

THE ANGELIC UNIVERSE OF JOHN DEE AND EDWARD KELLEY

The angelic or Enochian system of magic, includes:

1. The 48 Angelic Keys or Calls *(48 Claves Angelicae)*
A series of forty-eight invocations in the Angelic language with English translations (generated from the tables of the *Liber Loagaeth*) designed in part to open the Thirty Aires or Æthyrs, the celestial realms or heavens surrounding the physical world of the Four Elements in layers. Kelley sat at the Holy Table and the angel in the shewstone pointed with a rod to letters in the tables of the *Liber Loagaeth* that were identified only by a rank and column numbers. Dee looked at the appropriate Table, found the letter and wrote it down. The Calls were laboriously extracted in the Angelic Language, letter by letter, backwards from the end of each Call. This was necessary, because otherwise, as Dee explained in his diary on 12 April 1584, "… all things called would appear; and so hinder our proceeding in learning". [18] Later the angels provided English translations.

2. The Thirty Aires or Æthyrs
The term "Æthyrs" is used by the Golden Dawn and Aleister Crowley. It has been noted already that the Angel Nalvage described the Aires to Kelley as follows:

---

18. *T&FR*, p78.

"Understand therefore, that from the fire to the earth, there are 30 places or abidings: one above and beneath another." [19]

This is similar to the concept of descent of the Spirit (Fire) to Matter (Earth) through the Four Worlds of the Tree of Life of the Qabalah: namely, the Atziluthic World of the Spirit; the Briatic or Creative World; the Yetziratic or Formative World; and the Assiatic or Physical World of the Four Elements.[20] Here is a ready-made system for spiritual advancement and exploration that can be used in meditation and ritual using techniques similar to Pathworking and the "Rising-on-the-Planes" operations on the Tree of Life.

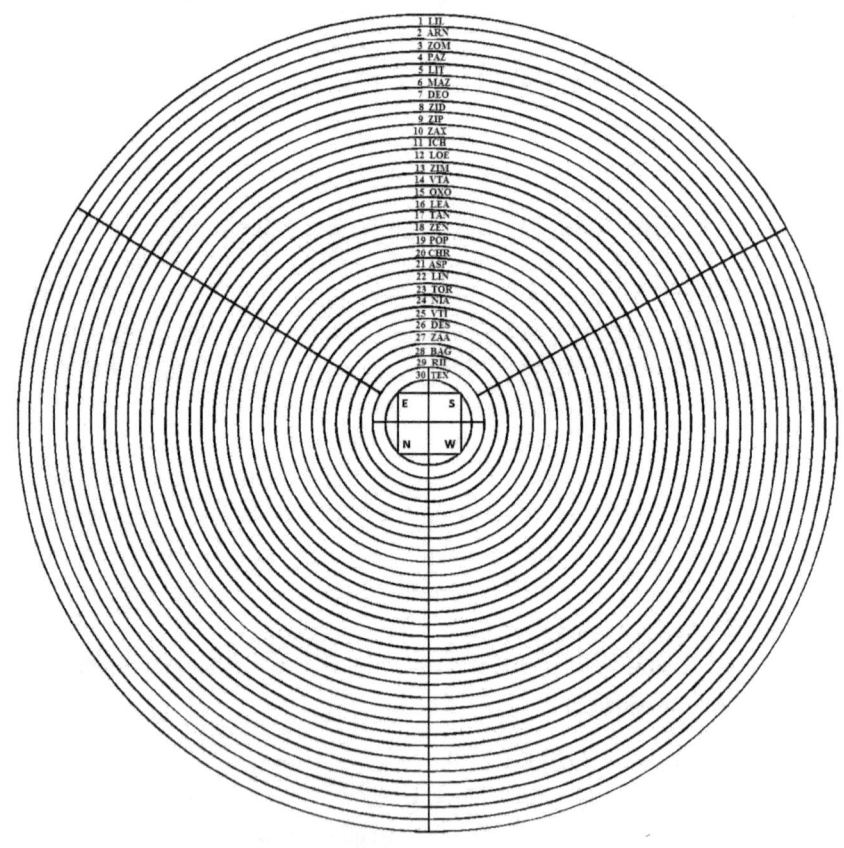

4. THE THIRTY AIRES or ÆTHYRS

---

19. Ibid., p.140.
20. The concept of the Four Worlds is explored further in Chapter 6.

Twelve Angelic Kings rule the Aires between them. They guide and protect one's travels in each Aire and must be treated with respect.

THE TWELVE ANGELIC KINGS

1. OLPAGED	7. ALPUDUS
2. ZIRACAH	8. CADAAMP
3. HONONOL	9. ZARZILG
4. ZARNAAH	10. LAVAVOT
5. GEBABAL	11. ZINGGEN
6. ZURCHOL	12. ARFALOG

Each Aire is governed by three Angelic Kings, except the Thirtieth Aire or TEX which has four, perhaps to reflect the spiritual aspect of the four quarters and the four elements. It is the closest Aire to the Earth and appears to form an etheric veil around the planet. The first Aire or LIL borders the super celestial world of the angels and archangels.

At the centre of the system are the Four Quarters or Watchtowers of the terrestrial world. These can be seen in the diagram above, positioned as in Dee's original drawing in his diary. Reading clockwise from the upper left is the Eastern Quarter; then the Southern Quarter; the Western; and finally, the Northern Quarter at the lower left. The table below shows the Thirty Aires their pronunciation and their Angelic Kings.

THE THIRTY AIRES and THEIR ANGELIC KINGS

1. LIL(Leel)	Zarzilg	Zinggen	Alpudus
2. ARN (Arn)	Zarnaah	Ziracah	Ziracah
3. ZOM (Zom)	Zarzilg	Alpudus	Lavavot
4. PAZ(Paz)	Lavavot	Lavavot	Arfaolg
5. LIT(Leet, Lit)	Olpaged	Alpudus	Zinggen
6. MAZ (Maz)	Gebabal	Arfaolg	Gebabal
7. DEO (Day-oh)	Zarnaah	Hononol	Zinggen
8. ZID(Zeed, Zid)	Gebabal	Olpaged	Zarzilg
9. ZIP(Zeep, Zip)	Hononol	Lavavot	Zarzilg
10. ZAX (Zaks)	Zinggen	Alpudus	Zarzilg
11. ICH(Eek)	Lavavot	Zurchol	Hononol
12. LOE(Lo-ay)	Zurchol	Cadaamp	Ziracah
13. ZIM(Zeem, Zim)	Lavavot	Olpaged	Alpudus

14. VTA(Oo-tah)	Gebabal	Alpudus	Arfaolg
15. OXO(Oh-kso)	Zarzilg	Lavavot	Arfaolg
16. LEA(Lay-ah)	Ziracah	Hononol	Arfaolg
17. TAN(Tan)	Ziracah	Olpaged	Zarzilg
18. ZEN(Zen)	Gebabal	Alpudus	Arfaolg
19. POP(Poh-puh)	Arfaolg	Cadaamp	Zinggen
20. CHR(Khar)	Gebabal	Hononol	Alpudus
21. ASP(Ahs-puh)	Arfaolg	Cadaamp	Zurchol
22. LIN(Leen, Lin)	Arfaolg	Olpaged	Arfaolg
23. TOR (Tor)	Zarnaah	Lavavot	Zinggen
24. NIA(Nee-ah)	Zarnaah	Lavavot	Zinggen
25. VTI(Oo-tee)	Zarnaah	Ziracah	Arfaolg
26. DES(Dess)	Arfaolg	Cadaamp	Arfaolg
27. ZAA(Zah-ah)	Ziracah	Zarnaah	Gebabal
28. BAG(Bah-guh)	Lavavot	Zarzilg	Zurchol
29. RII(Ree-ee)	Hononol	Zarnaah	Arfaolg
30. TEX(Teks)	Arfaolg Zarnaah	Hononol	Zurchol

Use the names of the Kings to help prevent straying from the path when travelling the Aires.

FUNCTION OF THE AIRES

Like the zodiac, the Aires affect the physical world which is divided into 91 areas of influence.

In theory entering a region on a spiritual or astral level will bring foresight of future events and, by working positive magic, influence can be wrought on troubled lands.

The angels of the Aires *"would bring in and again dispose Kings and all Governments upon Earth, and vary the Natures of things: with variation of every moment."* [21]

This is reminiscent of Heinrich Cornelius Agrippa, who wrote in Chapter XXXI of his *First Book of Occult Philosophy* (1531).

"He who knows how to compare divisions of provinces according to the Divisions of the Stars, with the Ministry of the Ruling Intelligences, and Blessings of the Tribes of Israel, the Lots of the Apostles, and Typical Seals of the Sacred Scripture, shall be able to obtain great and prophetical oracles, concerning every region, of things to come."

---

21. T&FR, p 140.

Dee later tabulated the 91 geographical parts of the earth with their ruling Aires, their divine names and sigils, and various correspondences (including spiritual servants and related Tribes of Israel) in *Liber Scientiae, Auxilii, et Victoriae Terrestris (The Book of Knowledge Help and Earthly Victory)*, dated 2 May 1585. (British Library Sloane MS 3191). However, these aspects are outside the scope of this work. For those interested, further details can be found in Lon Milo Duquette's *Enochian Vision Magick* (2008) and Geoffrey James's *Enochian Evocation of Dr John Dee* (2009).

3. The Great Table of Earth

In Krakow, on Wednesday, 20 June 1584, Edward Kelley's famous VISION OF THE FOUR CASTLES revealed that the four quarters or watchtowers of the physical world are governed by hierarchies of gods and angelic beings.
The text of the vision is as follows:

> *There appeared to him four very fair Castles, standing in the four parts of the world: out of which he heard the sound of a Trumpet.*
>
> *Then seemed out of every Castle a cloath to be thrown on the ground, of more than the breadth of a Table-cloth.*
>
> *Out of that in the East, the cloath seemed to be red, which was cast.*
>
> *Out of that in the South, the cloath seemed white.*
>
> *Out of that in the West, the cloath seemed green, with great knops on it.*
>
> *Out of that in the North, spread, or thrown out from the gate under foot, the cloath seemed to be very black.*
>
> *Out of every Gate then issued one Trumpeter, whose Trumpets were of strange form, wreathed, and growing bigger and bigger toward the end.*
>
> *After the Trumpeter followed three Ensign bearers.*
>
> *After them six ancient men, with white beards and staves in their hands.*
>
> *Then followed a comely man, with very much Apparel on his back, his Robe having a long train.*
>
> *After him came five men, carrying up of his train.*
>
> *Then followed one great Crosse, and about that four lesser Crosses.*
>
> *These Crosses had on them, each of them ten, like men, their faces distinctly appearing on the four parts of the Crosse, all over.*
>
> *After the Crosses followed 16 white Creatures.*

And after them, an infinite number seemed to issue, and to spread themselves orderly in a compasse, almost before the four foresaid Castles. [22]

John Dee made a sketch of Kelley's vision in his notebook.[23] A fine, but inaccurate, copy of the drawing features in *A True and Faithful Relation*. The corrected version is presented below.

Note the colours of the Quarters or Watchtowers. They are completely different from those assigned by the Order of the Golden Dawn. See Appendix I for further details. In Kelley's vision East is a "Fresh Red Cullor"; the South is "Lilly White"; the West is a "dark grene Cullor like garlik blades"; and the North is "blak as of bilbery juyce". These are the colours used for the building up the temples of the quarters from which to commence the travels in the Great Table Of Earth described later in this work. A gold talisman was subsequently made of this, but by neither Dee nor Kelley. It is now displayed in the British Museum along with Dee's wax discs and other magical equipment.[24]

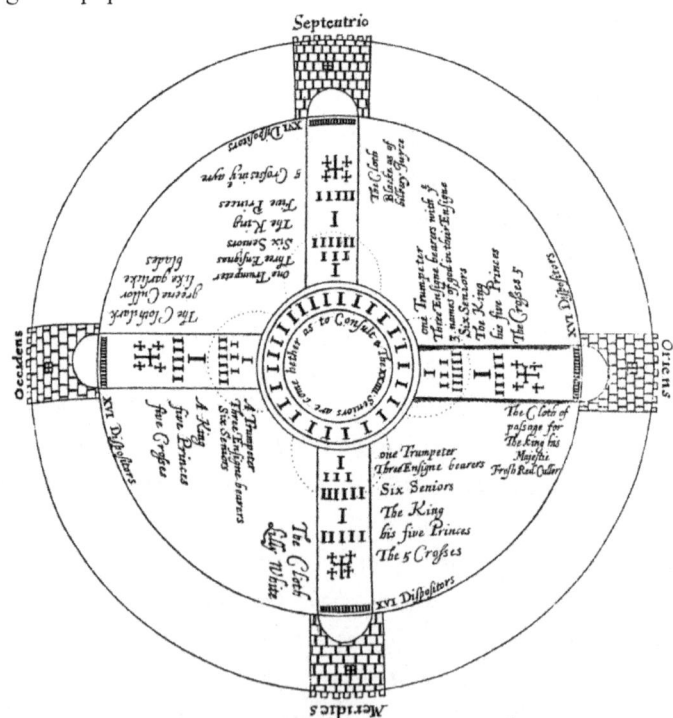

5. Edward Kelley's VISION OF THE FOUR CASTLES, 20TH June 1584
from *A True and Faithful Relation* and corrected according to British Library MS Cotton Appendix XLVI, Part I, folio 192v

4. The Physical World in Detail

The precise details of the hierarchies of angelic beings revealed by Kelley's Vision of 20 June 1584 slowly emerged during subsequent "actions". Later, the colour of each of the four quarters was further "expounded" by Kelley as follows:

The EASTERN Quarter is RED *"after new smitten Blood"*. The SOUTHERN Quarter is WHITE, *"Lilly-colour"*. The WESTERN Quarter is the GREEN of the *"skins of many Dragons, green: garlick- bladed"*. The NORTHERN Quarter is BLACK, *"Hair-coloured, Bilbery Juyce"*.[25]
These are not the "Elemental" colours specified by the Golden Dawn. Although valid, the Golden Dawn colours do not apply here, as the quarters are directional rather than elemental. They are not required when working the original system of Dee and Kelley. Please see Appendix I for further details.

The Vision then turned into a magical formula or Grid for the Four Quarters or Watchtowers filled with Latin letters forming the names of the Angelic Hierarchy of the Four Quarters. Angelic or Enochian characters were never used. The Golden Dawn added these.

EAST / SOUTH / NORTH / WEST

6. THE GREAT TABLE OF EARTH

22. *T&FR*, p. 168.   23. British Library MS Cotton Appendix XLVI, Part 1, fol. 92v.
24. The talisman was copied from the incorrect version printed in *T&FR* which jumbles up the colours of the quarters. Dee's original sketch is correct.   25. *T&FR*, p.171.

The internal design of the Watchtowers and the functions of their angels are the same for each quarter. However, the names of the angels and the aspect of the function will change according to the Quarter.

5. Structure of the Watchtowers

The Four Quarters or Watchtowers run clockwise from the Eastern Quarter (top left) and are bound together by what John Dee calls the GREAT (BLACK) CROSS or TABLET OF UNION:

Seen on diagram from the previous page:

EXARP   HCOMA   AMOCH   PRAXE (vertical)

MOTIB   ATNAN   NANTA   BITOM (horizontal)

Looking at each Watchtower in detail, note that each Quarter is divided into 4 Lesser or Sub-Angles containing a small cross (or a "Calvary Cross", as Dee termed it) positioned around a large equal-armed cross as follows. Here is the Eastern Quarter or Watchtower as an example.

1   **2**

r	Z	i	l	a	f	A	u	t	l	p	a
a	r	d	Z	a	i	d	p	a	L	a	m
c	z	o	n	s	a	r	o	Y	a	u	b
T	o	i	T	t	x	o	P	a	c	o	C
S	i	g	a	s	o	m	r	b	z	n	h
f	m	o	n	d	a	T	d	i	a	r	i
o	r	o	i	b	A	h	a	o	z	p	i
c	N	a	b	r	V	i	x	g	a	z	d
O	i	i	i	t	T	p	a	l	O	a	i
A	b	a	m	o	o	o	a	C	v	c	a
N	a	o	c	O	T	t	n	p	r	a	T
o	c	a	n	m	a	g	o	t	r	o	i
S	h	i	a	l	r	a	p	m	z	o	x

3   7. THE EASTERN WATCHTOWER   **4**

Lesser Angles: 1. Top Left   2. Top Right   3. Below Left   4. Below Right. From these Angel and God names are formed.

THE ANGELIC UNIVERSE OF JOHN DEE AND EDWARD KELLEY   29

The following are the most important. Be aware there are other names in the hierarchy of each Quarter that are not essential for this particular work.

EAST

r	Z	i	l	a	f	A	u	t	l	p	a
a	r	d	Z	a	i	d	p	a	L	a	m
c	z	o	n	s	a	r	o	Y	a	u	b
T	o	i	T	t	x	o	P	a	c	o	C
S	i	g	a	s	o	m	r	b	z	n	h
f	m	o	n	d	a	T	d	i	a	r	i
o	r	o	i	b	A	h	a	o	z	p	i
c	N	a	b	r	V	i	x	g	a	z	d
O	i	i	i	t	T	p	a	l	O	a	i
A	b	a	m	o	o	o	a	C	v	c	a
N	a	o	c	O	T	t	n	p	r	a	T
o	c	a	n	m	a	g	o	t	r	o	i
S	h	i	a	l	r	a	p	m	z	o	x

SOUTH

b	O	a	Z	a	R	o	p	h	a	R	a
u	N	n	a	x	o	P	S	o	n	d	n
a	i	g	r	a	n	o	o	m	a	g	G
o	r	p	m	n	i	n	g	b	e	a	L
r	s	O	n	i	z	i	r	l	e	m	U
i	z	i	n	r	C	z	i	a	M	h	L
M	O	r	d	i	a	l	h	C	t	G	A
R	O	c	a	n	c	h	i	a	s	o	M
A	r	b	i	z	m	i	i	l	p	i	Z
O	p	a	n	a	L	a	m	S	m	a	L
d	O	l	o	P	i	n	i	a	n	b	A
r	x	p	a	o	c	s	i	z	i	x	P
a	x	t	i	r	V	a	s	t	r	i	M

NORTH

d	o	n	p	a	T	d	a	n	V	a	a
o	l	o	a	G	e	o	o	b	a	v	a
O	P	a	m	n	o	O	G	m	d	n	m
a	p	l	s	T	e	d	e	c	a	o	p
s	c	m	i	o	o	n	A	m	l	o	x
V	a	r	s	G	d	L	b	r	i	a	p
o	i	P	t	e	a	a	p	D	o	c	e
p	s	u	a	c	n	r	Z	i	r	Z	a
S	i	o	d	a	o	i	n	r	z	f	m
d	a	l	t	T	d	n	a	d	i	r	e
d	i	x	o	m	o	n	s	i	o	s	p
O	o	D	p	z	i	A	p	a	n	l	i
r	g	o	a	n	n	P	A	C	r	a	r

WEST

T	a	O	A	d	u	p	t	D	n	i	M
a	a	b	c	o	o	r	o	m	e	b	B
T	o	g	c	o	n	x	m	a	l	G	M
n	h	o	d	D	i	a	l	e	a	o	C
p	a	t	A	x	i	o	V	s	P	s	N
S	a	a	i	x	a	a	r	V	r	o	l
m	p	h	a	r	s	l	g	a	i	o	L
M	a	m	g	l	o	i	n	L	i	r	X
o	l	a	a	D	a	g	a	T	a	p	A
p	a	L	c	o	i	d	x	P	a	c	N
n	d	a	z	N	Z	i	V	a	a	s	A
i	i	d	P	o	n	s	d	A	s	p	l
x	r	i	n	h	t	a	r	n	d	i	L

1. GOD NAME OF THE QUARTER

This runs across the centre of each Watchtower.
It consists of Three Names of 3, 4 and 5 Letters:(see diagram of the Quarters above)

East: ORO IBAH AOZPI
South: MOR DIAL HCTGA
West: MPH ARSL GAIOL
North: IOP TEAA PDOCE

2. GOOD ANGELS OF THE LESSER ANGLES

There are two groups of 4 Good Angels per Lesser or Sub-Angle, creating a total of 32 per Quarter. The first group is located:
(i) Above the Crossbar or Transversary of each Little Cross.

Functions:
SUB-ANGLE 1 • Combining of Natures
SUB-ANGLE 2 • Transportation from Place to Place
SUB-ANGLE 3 • Mechanical Arts
SUB-ANGLE 4 • Secrets of Mankind

The names are formed by rotating the letters of the name created by reading across the line above the transversary. Group (i) is included for information only and need not concern us. For full details, including the demonic angels or Cacodæmons of the Watchtowers, please see Lon Milo Duquette's *Enochian Vision Magick* (2008).

The second group of four good Angels is found
 (ii) Below the crossbar or transversary of each Little Cross.

Functions
SUB-ANGLE 1 • Medicine and Cure of Disease
SUB-ANGLE 2 • Virtues of Metals and Precious Stones
SUB-ANGLE 3 • Transformation
SUB-ANGLE 4 • Knowledge and Use of the Four Elements

The Angels governing the Elements in the fourth Sub-Angle are those needed for the meditational work. They help to form the base from which to explore the Æthyrs.

x	g	a	z	d
a	l	O	a	i
a	C	v	c	a
n	p	r	a	T
o	t	r	o	i
p	m	z	o	x

8. THE FOURTH SUB-ANGLE OF THE EASTERN WATCHTOWER

The names are formed by reading the letters across each line. Include central letter from cross if desired to increase effectiveness.

ACCA / ACUCA	for AIR
NPAT / NPRAT	for WATER
OTOI / OTROI	for EARTH
PMOX / PMZOX	for FIRE

The Angels are SUMMONED by the name in the vertical of the little Calvary Cross: AOVRRZ.

They are COMMANDED by the name in the crossbar or transversary of the little cross: ALOAI.

CHAPTER THREE

INVOCATIONS

There are 2 sets of Invocations to aid the scrying of the Great Table of Earth and the Aires. They are ideally utilised just before the meditation or pathworking in the Enochian realms.

1. *A Book of Supplications and Invocations*
Dee wrote this detailed workbook of prayers and invocations to all the Gods and Angels of the Watchtowers of the Great Table, but not for the malevolent spirits or Cacodæmons. However, as it contains neither a dismissal nor a license to depart, practitioners must close down the proceedings with care. According to the angel Ave, the angels from the Great Table should be invoked just the once and, when they had appeared, they would remain on call and forever obedient. Upon request, they would disappear until required once more. On Saturday, 30 June 1584, Dee explained the perpetual presence of the spirits to a disbelieving Edward Kelley and it is also the reason that a proper discharge was deemed unnecessary:

> "If you be obedient and humble, The Creatures of Heaven shall abide with you. Yea the Father and the Son, and the Holy Ghost shall make his dwelling with you. If you persevere, even with faith and humility, you shall see the wicked days that are to come, enjoy the promises of God, and be partaker of those blessed days that follow: For wonders unheard of, in, and of the world, are at hand. You are warned the Spirit of God rests with you."[26]

A Book of Supplication and Invocations is written in Latin and forms part of British Library MS Sloane 3191. It lacks a title page and the title derives from the first

---

26. T&FR, p.186

invocation, which is a fundamental supplication or prayer to God.[27] This is followed by invocations to all the Good Angels above and below the sixteen little Calvary Crosses of the four Watchtowers. The major problem with these invocations is that they are very longwinded, mainly because they were designed by Dee for his own use. A useful one is a *Fundamental Prayer to God and entreaty for the benign ministry of Good Angels* which, if it appeals, can precede the main ceremony for either working with the Four Elements or with the Aires. It will help prepare the participants for their journey into the angelic domain.

O JEHOVA ZEBAOTH, I invoke and implore most earnestly your Divine Power, Wisdom and Goodness (I, John Dee,[28] your unworthy servant), and most humbly and faithfully ask you to favour and assist me in all my works, words and cogitations, concerning, promoting or procuring your praise, honour and Glory. And by these your twelve mystical names ORO, IBAH, AOZPI, MOR, DIAL, HCTGA, OIP, TEAA, PDOCE, MPH, ARSL, GAIOL, most ardently do I entreat and implore your Divine and Omnipotent Majesty: that all your faithful Angelic Spirits whose mystical names are expressed in this book and whose offices are briefly noted, in whatever part of the world they be and, in whatever time of my life they are summoned by (the said John) by means of their peculiar powers or authority of your Holy Name (likewise contained in this book), that most swiftly they come to me (the aforesaid John) visible, affable, and appear to me peacefully and remain with me visibly according to my wishes, and that they disappear at my request from me and from my sight. And through you and that reverence and obedience which they owe you in those twelve mystical names above mentioned, that they give satisfaction amicably to me also (the said John), at each and every moment in my life, and in each and every deed or request to all, some or one of them, and to do this quickly, well, completely and perfectly to discharge, perfect and complete all this according to their virtues and power both general and individual and through the injunctions given them by you (O God) and their charged offices and ministry. AMEN.

Through you, JESUS CHRIST,
AMEN.[29]

---

27. Translations can be found in Geoffrey James's *Enochian Magick of Dr John Dee* (San Francisco: Red Wheel/Weiser, 2009) or by Christopher Upton in Robert Turner's *Elizabethan Magic* (Shaftesbury, Dorset: Element Books, 1989), now out of print.

Jehovah Tzabaoth (IHVH TzBAVTh) or the Lord of Hosts is the god associated with the Sephira Netzach on the Qabalistic Tree of Life. The name defines God as the supreme commander over all heavenly forces; a God who is transcendent, exalted and omnipotent and, therefore, quite appropriate here. If the above invocation is felt to be too cumbersome and overloaded with Christian references, the following abridgement could be considered as a possible alternative or as a guide to one's own composition.

JEHOVAH TZABAOTH
We invoke most earnestly and call upon your divine power, wisdom and goodness. And through these your Twelve Mystical Names

ORO IBAH AOZPI
MOR DIAL HCTGA
MPH ARSL GAIOL (GAI-OL)
OIP TEAA PDOCE

We conjure and pray that your angelic spirits may be called forth from any and all parts of the universe,
Let them come most swiftly
And depart peacefully upon request;
And let them give reverence and obedience before thy Twelve Mystical Names, fulfilling all that is asked of them according to their virtues and powers.

JEHOVAH TZABAOTH
We thank thee.
AMEN

The invocation to the various angels of the Four Elements in the fourth lesser angle of each of the four Watchtowers is equally as tortuous, but it is still quite potent and may be employed if preferred. Here follows the *Address to the Four Angels of the East, each of whom understands all the living creatures of one Element and their uses.* This invocation can be used for the Elemental Angels of the other quarters by simply changing the names accordingly.

---

28. Insert the name of the operator here. 29. Translation by Christopher Upton in *Elizabethan Magic* (1989), p.64

O you Angels, full of the truth and goodness of God (you I say), ACCA or ACUCA, NPAT or NPRAT, OTOI or OTROI, and PMOX or PMZOX, who have authority in the eastern part of the world such that each of you has your particular gift or office, peculiar skill, knowledge, power and authority in each of the Four Elements or matrices of the world.

O you ACCA, or ACUCA, eminent Angel that perceives all the diverse species of living creatures in all the eastern air and perfectly understands for what uses to mankind they were created by God; you also illustrious NPAT or NPRAT, who understands the species and true use of the living creatures in all the eastern waters; and you famous OTOI, or OTROI, that exactly comprehends the various species that enjoy life in all the eastern land and for what uses they were created by God; and finally you PMOX, or PMZOX, shining Angel of God, that has cognition fully of the vital properties, most secret and efficacious, of the eastern fire.

O you all (I say), faithful ministers of our God and maker, who, in the eastern part of the world, understand these and many other secrets and mysteries of the Four Elements, granted, assigned and deputed to your knowledge and offices by our Omnipotent maker, and are able to impart and clearly communicate such secrets (with God's approval) to us (called and elected by the living heavenly voice) to the praise honour and glory of God and through your own great charity to the human race.

Therefore, I John Dee[30], most ardent lover and seeker, after secrets of this kind (and that particularly for the praise, honour and glory of our God) in the name of that God and our maker, humbly supplicate you that I have named, both individually and together, trustfully seek and require you, by the Holy Names of our God AOVRRZ and ALOAI, willingly and entirely to fulfil, benignly to grant clearly to enact and lovingly to accomplish the completion, achievement and execution, both plain, entire and perfect (after this hour) that I should ask and seek the helpful presence and personal appearance of all or one of you, such petitions as concern and entail your said particular offices and gifts or your special knowledge and power, by these Holy Names of God AOVRRZ and ALOAI, AMEN.

Through these revered and mystical names of God,
AOVRRZ and ALOAI,
AMEN. [31]

---

30. Insert the name of the operator here.
31. Translation by Christopher Upton in *Elizabethan Magic* (1989), p.73.

Understandably, many will prefer to write their own invocations, while others will simply adapt Dee's texts to suit themselves. If writing one's own for the *Knowledge and Use of the Four Elements*, make sure to include the four Elemental Angels of the Quarters concerned, and the appropriate summoning and commanding Lesser Gods from the Calvary Cross of the Sub-Angle. Incorporating the God Name of the Quarter concerned, as in the example below, may also increase the effectiveness of the invocation, which in this case, is to the God of the Eastern Quarter.

ORO IBAH AOZPI

O mighty God of the East, we pray in thy three holy names to guide us through thy lesser fourth angle, that we may open our consciousness and gain insight of the Four Elements of The East, so enabling us to deploy their virtues for the good of all.
Amen

The invocations to the four elemental angels follow. Full details of the ritual can be found in Chapter Eleven.

2. *CLAVES ANGELICÆ* - The Angelic Keys Or Calls

A total of 48 Calls or Keys (the *Claves Angelicæ*) comprise the second set of invocation. They were received in the Angelic Language, before Dee and Kelley actually received details of the Aires and the Great Table of Earth.

Dee does not specify the use of the first 18 Calls, which has lead to much speculation, and many, including Aleister Crowley and the Golden Dawn have arbitrarily assigned them to the four Watchtowers and their sixteen Sub-angles. However, there is no evidence for this.

However, Calls19 to 48 relate directly to each of the 30 Aires, making them ideal to use as an invocation for the Aires. Termed the *Cry of the Æthyrs* by Aleister Crowley, it is basically the same Key; that is, Call 19, with the name and number of the relevant Aire being inserted for Calls 20 to 48.

Edward Kelley: "Now change the Name, and the Call is all one", and Dee notes in the margin, "How this One Call may serve the 30." [32]

However, the Calls immediately create two problems for the scryer.

I: LANGUAGE

The Calls are in the Angelic Language, also known as Enochian. It is from them, that the bulk of the language derives. Nevertheless, this is modern problem.

32. *T&FR*, p. 209.

Enochian letters were never put on the Great Table of Earth by Dee and Kelley. This is a later development. In fact, as Enochian is read from right to left, so indeed should be the names of the Gods and Angels on the Great Table if they are transliterated into Enochian. As John Dee remarks:

"... in my mynde it semeth requisite that as all the writing and reding of that holy language is from the right hand to the left, So the begynning of the boke must be, (as it were in respect of our most usuall manner of bokes, in all languages of latin, greke, english and c.) at the ende of the boke: and the ende, at the begynning, as in the hebru bible."[33]

This makes a nonsense of Enochian lettered Great Tables with the names still reading left to right.

Fortunately for us, Dee wanted English translations for the Keys, and the angels willingly obliged On 2 July 1584, when he was told would receive the Keys in English in a few days, he was grovelling grateful:

Ave [Angel]:"You shall have those Calls in English on Thursday. And so ask me no more questions".

Dee:"Thanks, honour, and glory, be to our Creator, Redeemer, And Sanctifier, now and ever, Amen."[34]

For those of us who are not polyglots with a fluency in the Holy Language, it will be best to make the call in English or one's first language and follow it by the Enochian version. Although it might seem glamorous to recite it purely in Enochian, it is totally pointless if mispronounced and without any idea of what is being said. Further information on the Angelic Language, including the alphabet can be found in Appendix III.

II: PRONUNCIATION

The language is allegedly the speech of Angels - so how does one pronounce it? A basic guide now follows.

Dee broke the words into syllables similar to English, but sometimes pronounced letters individually with "z" sometimes being "zod" in a few instances.

The Golden Dawn injected a system based on the Hebrew vowel system to deal

---

33. Peterson, Joseph, ed. *John Dee's Five Books of Mysteries*, p.411.
34. *T&FR*, p.189.

with consonant clusters, resulting in every letter being pronounced. Sometimes the use was not consistent and was extremely awkward and unwieldy.

For example, "LIL", the First Aire, is pronounced "Leel" according to Dee's diaries, but by the Golden Dawn method it would be "El-ee-el". Dee made several notes during the reception of the Calls that can help with the pronunciation of the names of the angels and reading the Call of the Æthyrs. To overcome the problem, perhaps devise a pronunciation of one's own. If it sounds good to you, it probably will to the angels as well. Three versions of the Angelic Key of the Thirty Aires now follow: the English translation provided by the Angels, the original Angelic or Enochian version, and a Phonetic Angelic rendering. Dee also indicated where the stress falls in each word. In the phonetic angelic version below, the stress is emphasised by bold type. The majority of the letters are pronounced as in English. The most important exceptions are these. Examples are taken from the Key and their location within the Call is indicated by the line number.

C = S before **I** and **E** (with exceptions) and in consonant clusters. For example, **Noncf** is pronounced **nonsuf** (lines 4, 5), but **nonca** is pronounced **nonsa** (line 2).

CH = K See **Chis (kis)**, lines 1,3; **Christeós (Kristeos)**, lines 7,10,12; **ovcho (ov-ko)**, line 9; **unchi (un-ki)** line 17; **orócha (oro-ka)**, line23.

G = J before **I** and **E** See **caósgi (caosji)** , lines 4,7; **DG** in consonant clusters and when the final letter of a word. See **Ag (adg)**, lines 10,12; **tonug (tonudg)**, line 15; **Levithmong (Levith-mondg)**, line 16; **faórgt (fa-ordgt)**, line 21; **qting (ka-tindg)**,line 26; **cácrg (ka-kurdg)**, line 28.

Y/I = Y often at beginning of words. See **Iaída (Ya-i-da)**, line1; **iáodaf (Ya-o-daf)** line 6; **Iadnămad (Yad-na-mad)**, line 31, but note **Idoigo** (Id-we-go), line 6.

For readers interested in studying the Angelic Language further, see *The Angelical Language* by Aaron Leitch (2010) and *The Complete Enochian Dictionary* by Donald C. Laycock (2001).

CHAPTER FOUR

THE CALLS OF THE ÆTHYRS

THE ANGELIC KEY OF THE THIRTY ÆTHYRS (English)[35]

1. Oh you hevens, which dwell in [TEX the thirtieth Aire][36], are Mighty in the partes of the Erth, and execute the Judgement of the highest:

2. To you it is sayd,

3. Beholde the face of your God, the begynning of comfort: whose eyes are the brightne's of the hevens:

4. Which provided you for the government of the Erth, and her unspeakable varieties,

5. Furnishing you with a power understanding, to dispose all things

6. According to the providence of Him that sitteth on the Holy Throne; and rose up in the begynning, saying,

7. The Earth, let her be governed by her parts, and Let there be Division in her, that the glory of her may be allwayes drunken and vexed in itself:

8. Her course, let it runne with the hevens: and as a handmayd let her serve them:

9. One season, let it confound an other:

10. And let there be no Creature uppon, or within her, the same:

11. All her members, let them differ in their qualities:

[35] Transcribed from British Library Sloane MS. 3191 preserving Dee's original spelling, punctuation, capitalisation and diacritical marks in both the English and the Angelic version.
[36] Enter the appropriate name and number of the Aire or Æthyr.

12. And let there be no one Creature equall with an other:

13. The reasonable Creatures of Erth, Let them vex and weede out one an other:

14. And the dwelling places, Let them forget their names:

15. The work of Man, and his pomp, Let them be defaced.

16. His buyldings, let them become Caves for the beasts of the field:

17. Confound her understanding, with darkness.

18. For why?

19. It repenteth me I made Man.

20. One while Let her be known, and another while a stranger:

21. Bycause she is the bed of a Harlot, and the dwelling place of him that is fal[le]n:

22. Oh you hevens, arise,

23. The lower hevens underneath you, Let them serve you:

24. Govern those that govern:

25. Cast down, such as fall:

26. Bring forth with those that encrease: and destroy the rotten:

27. No place let remayne in one number:

28. Ad[d] and diminish untill the stars be numbered:

29. ARRISE, MOVE, and APPERE before the Covenant of his mouth, which he hath sworn unto us, in his Justice:

30. OPEN the Mysteries of your Creation:

31. And make us partakers of undefyled knowledge.

THE CALL OF THE ÆTHYRS (Angelic)

1. Madríax ds praf [TEX]³⁷ , chis Micaólz saánir Caósgo, od físis bal zizras Iaída!

2. Nonca gohúlim:

3. Micma adoían MAD, iáod bliorb, Såbaooáŏna chis Lucíftîas perípsol;

4. Ds abraása noncf netááib Caosgi, od tilb adphaht dámploz,

5. Toóat noncf gmicálzŏma, Lrásd tófglo

6. Marb yárry IDOIGO od torzulp iáodaf, go hól.

7. Caósgi, tabaord saánir, od Christéós yrpóil tióbl, Busdir tilb noaln paid orsba od dodrmni zylna.

8. Elzáptilb, parm gi perípsax, od ta qurlst booapiS.

9. L nibm, ovcho symp,

10. Od Christeós Ag tol torn mirc q tióbl LeL,

11. Ton paombd, dilzmo aspían.

12. Od Christeós Ag L tortorn parach a symp,

13. Cordziz, dodpal od fifalz Ls-mnad,

14. Od fargt, bams omaóas,

15. Conísbra od avăvox, tonug,

16. Ors cat bl, noăsmi tabgés, Levithmong.

17. Vnchi omp tilb ors.

18. Bagle?

19. Mooóăh ol córdziz.

20. L capímăo ixomaxip, od ca cócasb gosăa.

---

37. Enter the appropriate name of the Aire or Æthyr.

21. Baglen pi tianta abábǎlond, od faórgt teloc vo-vim.

22. Mádrǐiax, torzu.

23. Oádriax orócha, abóǎpri.

24. Tabáǒri priáz ar ta bas.

25. A dí pan cor sta dobix.

26. Yolcam priázi ar coazior, Od quasb qting.

27. Ripír paoxt sa gá cor.

28. Uml od prdzar, cácrg Aoivéǎe corumpt.

29. TORZV, ZACAR, od ZAMRAN aspt sibsi butmǒna, ds surzas tia baltan.

30. Odo cicle Qáa:

31. Od Ozazma plapli Iadnǎmad.

THE CALL OF THE ÆTHYRS (Phonetic Angelic) [38]

1. Madri-yax di-es praf [TEX][39], kis Mi-**ca**-olz sa-a-nir Ka-**os**-go, Od **fi**-sis bal-**ziz**-ras Ya-**i**-da!

2. Nonsa go-**hu**-lim:

3. Mikma ado-**i**-an MAD, **ya**-od bliorb, Saba-o-o-**ay**-ona kis Lu-**sif**-ti-as pe-**rip**-sol

4. Di-es abra-**a**ssa nonsuf ne-**ta**-a-ib Ka-**os**-ji, od tilb ad-faht dam-ploz,

5. To-**o**-at nonsuf gmi-**cal**-zoma, el-rasd **tof**-glo,

6. Marb yarry ID-WE-GO od tor-zulp ya-**o**-daf, go-hol:

7. Ka-**os**-gi, **ta**ba-ord sa-**a**-nir, od Kris-te-**os** yr-**po**-il ti-obl, bus-dir tilb no-aln pa-**id** ors-ba od dod-rum-ni zylna.

8. El-**zap**-tild, parm-gi pe-**rip**-sax, od ta kurlst boo-apis.

9. El-ni-bm, **ov**-ko symp;

10. Od Kristeos adg Tolt-torn mirk ka ti-**obl** LeL,

11. Ton pa-ombt, dilz-mo as-**pi**-an,

12. Od Kris-**te**-os Adg el Tol-torn **pa**-rach a-symp,

13. Cord-ziz dod-pal od fi-falz els-menad,

14. Od far-gad, bams oma-**o**-as.

15. Co-**nis**-bra od A-va-vox, to-nudge.

16. Ors-**cat**-bel, no-**as**-mi tab-jes Levith-mondg.

17. Un-ki omp-tilb ors.

18. Ba-gle?

19. Mo-o-**o**-ah ol Cord-ziz.

---

38. See *T&FR*, p201-208 for Dee's pronunciation upon which this is based.
39. Enter the appropriate name of the Aire or Æthyr.

20. El capi-**may**-o ix-o-max-ip, od ca-**co**-casb, go-**sa**-a.

21. Baglen pi-**i ti**-an-ta a ba-**ba**-lond, od fa-**ordge** teloch-vo-vim.

22. Madri-yax, tor-zu!

23. O-**adri**-yax oro-ka, abo-ap-ri.

24. Taba-**o-ri pri**-az art-a-**bas**.

25. A-**dir**-pan, cor-sta dobix.

26. Yol-cam pri-a-zi ar-co-a-zior. Od kwasb ka-tindge.

27. **Ri**-pir pa-a-oxt sa-**ga**-kor.

28. Vm-el od purd-**zar**, ka-kurg A-oi-**ve**-ee corumpt.

29. TOR-ZU, ZACAR, od ZAMRAN aspt Sib-si but-mo-na, di-es sur-zas tia baltan:

30. Odos sik-le **ka**-a,

31. Od O-zaz-ma plap-li Yad-**na**-mad.

CHAPTER FIVE

GUIDE TO THE OPERATION

The Temple or Sacred Workplace
Everyone has their own preferred way of working. Many sources detail all kinds of temples from the simple minimalist working space to those festooned with ceremonial furnishings, including meticulously painted Enochian tablets, and consecrated by elaborate ceremonies. On one occasion, in the Algerian desert, Crowley's "temple" was no more than a circle of rocks (see Appendix I) – quite a simple affair compared to some of his other places of working.

Nevertheless, whatever form the temple takes, it is essential that the area is cleansed in order to create a sacred space in which to work. Even John Dee himself was reminded of this. On 15 November 1583, when in Lübeck, North Germany, he was told by a disembodied voice, claiming to be the *"Spirit of Truth and Understanding"*, that this spirit

"will not be dasht in pieces with worldlings; neither use I to dwell in defiled places – for my sanctuary is holy and my Gates are without spot. And with me, there dwelleth no unrightousnesse." [40]

Dee often spoke of going to his oratory, indicating that he had a designated chamber of practice and he once spoke of converting a spare bedroom in Mortlake to that effect. There are no descriptions of the house in Kraków that Dee rented. It was located in St Stephen's Square (Plac Szczepański) and it was here that Dee and Kelley received details of the Thirty Æthyrs, the Angelic Keys and the structure of the Great Table of Earth. The house was later rebuilt, but in 1908 it was demolished and Art Nouveau apartments built on the site. [41]

40. *T&FR*, p. 50.

However, in Prague, a detailed description survives of the room Dee and Kelley used for their angelic communications in the house of Tadeáš Hájek z Hájku (1525-1600), the Imperial Physician at the court of the Emperor Rudolf II. The house was in Betlémské Náměstí (Bethlehem Square) and they stayed there between August 1584 and January 1985. The house was demolished in 1896, but a photograph survives from 1870.

9. Hájek's House (Land Registry number: čp252), 1870 (Photographer unknown).[42]

---

41. For further information see *John Dee and Edward Kelley in Cracow: Identifying the House of Enochian Revelations* by Rafal T. Prinke and Kamila Follprecht, *Polish Journal of the Arts and Culture*, no.13 (1/2015), pp. 119-136. Also online at http://www.pjac.uj.edu.pl/documents/30601109/fd846ad7-618b-4ad9-90eb-fc352f6e718e. 42. See also Appendix V.

The house also features in a drawing of 1869 by Czech artist Antonín Josef Levý (1845- 1897).

On Wednesday, 15 August 1584, Dee gives a detailed account of the little chamber in his diary:

"We began on the day of the assumption of the BlessedVirgin Mary: in the excellent little Stove or Study of D[octor] Hajeck ... which Study seemed in times past (Anno 1518) to have been the Study of some student, or A[lchemist] skillfull of the holy stone: a name was in divers places of the Study, noted in letters of Gold and Silver, Simon Baccalaureus Pragensis ..."

10. Antonín Levý. *Betlémské Náměstí*. 1869 (detail) [43]

The room, in fact, had been the study of Hájek's father, Šimon Bakalar called Hájek (1485-1551), who became a Baccalaureate of Prague University in 1509. An expert alchemist, Šimon was the author of the first book in the Czech language and a renowned collector of religious literature. He had adorned the whole room with *"very many Hieroglyphical Notes Philosophical, in Birds, Fishes, Flowers, Fruits, Leaves, and sixVessels, as for the Philosophers works."*

---

43. Public domain via Wikipedia Commons.

Over the door was this verse:
Undying honour and equal glory are due to him
By whose genius this wall is of many colours.

The wall on the south side bore an allegorical account (in Latin) of the spiritual transformation of the adept, which paralleled on a higher plane the striving for the physical transmutation of metal into gold in the alchemical laboratory.

If a fair woman is married to a ruddy husband, soon they are united: they are held together by an embrace. They themselves will dissolve; without help, when they are ready. As they had been two, so they become one in body. [44] *In the beginning there are two things, the Sun together with the Moon. However, in the lower world, it follows - you will see - the stone also comes from these things.*

The Sun perfects the power of the Moon by a motion in things. The Sun goes to the Moon through the middle and creates one thing. The Sun opens sail and passes through the eclipsed heavens. He runs, when the Moon runs back exalted afresh, because she herself may now give light, which is held fast in the Sun. Nor has the Sun truly gone away, but wishes to remain: illuminating clearly the defunct body assuredly.

If you were to gain knowledge from things, you would discover what was to be. This Art is precious, exact, elusive and rare. Our Art is a game for the boy, the work of women. Know, all sons of this Art, that no-one can gather the fruit of our elixir, except by entering our elemental stone; even if he seeks another way, he will never enter nor embrace it. Rubigo[45] *is the work, because it is made from gold alone, when once it has entered into its own humidity.* [46]

"And so it ended." [47]

---

44. The male and female are now combined in one body creating the alchemical hermaphrodite or "Rebis". The term features occasionally in the original Latin inscription (see Appendix V). It is the first stage of the alchemical process and is the coming together (Conjunctio) of opposing archetypal forces of male and female (the Red King and White Queen) or the Sun and the Moon.
45. Literally "rust". In alchemy, this is a substance transformed to a state of redness. The process is known as "rubification".
46. A similar statement can be found in the *Turba Philisophorum or Assembly of Philosophers*, one of the oldest European alchemy texts, possibly written c. 900 A.D. It is organized into 72 Dictums. The *46th Dictum* includes the statement: *Rubigo is according to the work, because it is from gold alone*.
47. T&FR, p. 212. Translated by Barbara Prichard. The wall inscription was in Latin and is transcribed from Dee's diaries in Appendix V.

Local legend relates that Edward Kelley had a dedicated sacred space at the top of the tower of his house in Prague. After Dee had returned to Britain in 1589 following the collapse of their partnership, Kelley briefly prospered from his alleged alchemical skills. He received a knighthood from the Emperor Rudolf II in February 1590[48] and bought property in Prague, supposedly including the tower house in the shadow of the castle, although there is no evidence for this. Located at 8 Jánský Vršek, the house is known as The Donkey in the Cradle (U Osla v Kolébce).

The strange name is explained by a story involving Kelley who was said to regularly star-gaze from a room at the top of the tower, which also served as his alchemical laboratory. One stormy night a woman, who lived in the building, saw his lack of ears. He promptly cursed her, giving her baby the head of a donkey. The full legend can be found in Appendix VI, together with information about Kelley's ears. At the time of writing, the house is currently a boutique hotel with an alchemical themed bar, the Kellyxír. The property also houses a small hermetic museum – *The Museum of Alchemists and Magicians of Old Prague*.

11. Kelley's Tower, Prague. (Photograph © R.E. Cousins)

---

48. Some sources give the earlier date of June 1589.

Creating a Sacred Space

To achieve a sacred space "without a spot" suitable for John Dee's grumpy "Spirit of Truth and Understanding", first delineate the working area by placing a light or candle in each of the four quarters. While ordinary plain white candles are satisfactory, for greater effect use coloured lights appropriate to the quarter as detailed in Edward Kelley's *Vision of the Four Castles*, namely: Red in the East, White in the South, Green in the West, and Black or Bilberry Purple in the North. Use coloured candles and/or candle holders. The white light of the South can be achieved with white candle in a clear glass holder and the black light of the North with a black candle or a deep purple glass holder.

Once the temple space is established, burn some incense or light a joss-stick (Frankincense is a good all-round choice) and proceed to cleanse the place with some basic preparatory rituals.

Begin by performing the Qabalistic Cross thus.
Stand facing East, then using a black-handled dagger or the first two fingers of the right hand

1. Touch the forehead saying ATEH [Ah teh] (Thou art).
2. Touch the breast and say MALKUTH) [Mahl-kooth] (the Kingdom).
3. Touch the right shoulder and say VE-GEBURAH [Vay-geb-or-rah] (and the Power).
4. Touch the left shoulder and say VE GEDULAH [Vay-ged-you-lah] (and the Glory).
5. Clasp hands together on the breast and say LE-OLAM, AMEN [Lay-orh-lahm, Ar-men] (to the Ages, Amen).

Visualise the cross in brilliant white, blazing light, drawn from on high.
Follow this by a short prayer known as the 'Binding of the Qliphoth'. It has been adapted from *The Key Of Solomon* and is employed to bind or render impotent any adverse or negative forces that may be present. This binding ritual can precede any magical operation and is particularly helpful for those involving the invocation or evocation of spirits. It is, therefore, ideal to use before summoning the angels of the Great Table and /or the Angelic Kings of the Thirty Aires or Æthyrs.

Having completed the Qabalistic Cross, now recite aloud the Binding of the Qliphoth:

When we enter herein with all humility, let God the Almighty One enter into this place, by the entrance of an eternal happiness, of a Divine prosperity, of a perfect joy, of an abundant charity, and of an eternal salutation.

Let all the demons fly from this place, ESPECIALLY THOSE WHO ARE OPPOSED UNTO THIS WORK, and let the angels of peace assist and protect this place / circle, from which let discord and strife fly and depart.

Magnify and extend upon me / us, O Lord, thy most holy name, (and bless our conversation and our assembly.)[49] Sanctify, O Lord, my / our humble entry herein, thou the Blessed and Holy One of the Eternal Ages.

Amen.[50]

Finish by repeating the Qabalistic Cross.

Note "this place" also designates one's own body as well as the working area. When spirits are to be summoned, as in these Enochian workings, this rite must be followed by the Lesser Banishing Ritual of the Pentagram which will powerfully cleanse the atmosphere and dispel all evil magnetism, demonic forms and impure thought-forms from the temple or place of operation.

Lesser Banishing Ritual of the Pentagram

As with the Qabalistic Cross visualise, the pentagrams in brilliant white fire.

1. Stand with feet together facing east.

2. Perform the Qabalistic Cross. The repetition of the cross reinforces the protection.

3. Inscribe in the air with an outstretched right arm the banishing pentagram either with the dagger of the Art or the index finger.

4. Begin at the bottom left point and when back again at the starting point, continue up to the apex of the pentagram in order to seal it and then immediately downwards to its centre. Stab the central point with the dagger or index finger and vibrate the God Name IHVH [Ye-ho-vah].

---

49. Include if there is more than one participant.
50. Adapted from the *The Key of Solomon the King (Clavicula Salomomis)*,tr. and ed. by S .Liddell MacGregor Mathers (London: Routledge and Kegan Paul, 1981), p. 18.

5. Keeping the arm extended, turn to the South and draw the pentagram in the same fashion, stab the centre and vibrate the God Name ADNI [Ah-doh-nye].

6. Now turn to the West and repeat the process and vibrate the God Name AHIH [Eh-he-yay].

7. Turn to the North, repeat and vibrate the God Name AGLA [Ah-gla].

8. Keeping the arm outstretched, return to the East to complete the circle.

9. Next, stand in the form of the pentagram with the feet apart and the arms extended sideways.

Now invoke the archangels.
Before me, RAPHAEL [Rah-fay-el]
Behind me, GABRIEL [Gab-ray-el]
On my right hand, MICHAEL [Mee-kay-el]
On my left hand, AURIEL [Oh-ray-el]
About me flame the Pentagrams
And above me shines the six-rayed star (see a blazing hexagram above).

10. Conclude with the Qabalistic Cross.

Visualise the four Archangels of the Elements as huge, towering figures. As they are protecting the participants from adverse forces, they will be looking out from the circle with their backs towards the operator.

• In the East, Raphael, the Archangel of Air, wears robes in flashing colours of yellow and amethyst. He holds the Air Dagger.

• In the South, Michael, the Archangel of Fire, is robed in red and green. He holds a flaming sword pointing upwards or alternatively a wand or staff (for controlling the fire).

• In the West, Gabriel, the Archangel of Water, has blue and orange robes. He bears a great cup from which water flows.

• In the North, Auriel, the Archangel of Earth, is clad in robes of citrine, olive, russet and black and holds aloft a pentacle bearing a hexagram, like so.

The Rite

With the ritual space now cleansed, remain facing East and say the following adoration:

> *Holy art Thou, Lord of the Universe,*
> *Holy art Thou, whom Nature hath not formed,*
> *Holy art Thou, the vast and mighty One,*
> *Lord of the Light and of the Darkness.*

Next perform the Opening Sign or the Rending of the Veil as follows
• Stand with both arms outstretched in front of you with the palms of the hands together.
• Turn the hands so the backs of the hands are now together.
• Move the arms to the side as if parting curtains or drapery.
• Make the proclamation:
I DECLARE THE TEMPLE OF THE ENOCHIAN REALMS OPEN.
You are now treading on Holy Ground, so proceed in due honour and reverence to the Gods and angels.

It is now time to enter the inner mystical space of the Enochian temple in order to commence the working with the Four Elements or the Æthyrs. At this point make a general invocation to the gods to help prepare for the journey through the angelic domain. It has been suggested in Chapter Three that John Dee's *Fundamental Prayer to God*, or one's own version of this, could be a suitable preparatory invocation. An effective alternative to consider is the *Qabalistical Invocation to Solomon* from Éliphas Lévi's *Transcendental Magic: its Doctrine and Ritual*, translated by Arthur Edward Waite in 1896. An earlier rendering of Lévi's French original can be found at the end of Mather's edition of the *Key of Solomon* (first published in 1888). The original French version and a new English translation of this together with a short article can be found in Appendix IV of this work.

After the invocation, pause and meditate a moment as you are now in your mystic Temple. In the spirit vision, subtly adjust the design of the temple in order to reflect whether an Elemental or an Aire working is being undertaken. In either case the door to the Enochian realms is before you. If desired, the build-up of the temple can commence while making the general invocation.

Elemental Workings

Visualise the entire room or temple - walls, floor, and ceiling - in the correct colour of the quarter being explored - i.e. red for the East, white for the South, green for the West and black or deep purple for the North. Work facing the appropriate direction and commence the operation with the Eastern Quarter and continue clockwise through each cardinal points in turn. See the door to the Enochian worlds ahead. The four elemental signs are graven on the door one beneath the other in the order given in Dee's diaries.

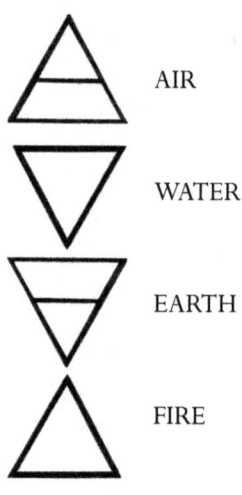

12. The Elemental Signs

Using the Eastern Quarter as an example, contemplate the door and invoke the God of the East as follows:

ORO IBAH AOZPI

O mighty God of the East, we pray in thy three holy names to guide us through thy lesser fourth angle, that we may open our consciousness and gain insight of the Four Elements of The East, so enabling us to deploy their virtues for the benefit of all. Amen.

Move towards the Red Door to the world of the Elements of the East.

The door becomes transparent.

Pass through. There is a mist before you

GUIDE TO THE OPERATION

Stand on the other side and invoke in turn the four Angels of the Elements to reveal the elemental world of the East.
The Elemental Angels run downwards from the cross-bar in the fourth sub-angle:
ACCA for AIR
NPAT for WATER
OTOI for EARTH
PMOX for FIRE
These angels are summoned by AOVRRZ, commanded by ALOAI whose names are found in the Calvary Cross within the subangle.

Invocation

Through the holy names of this lesser angle
AOVRRZ [a-o-ur-rez]
ALOAI [a-lo-ay]
We invoke thee, Angels of the East, so that each one of thee may reveal to us thy elemental domain, the creatures living therein and their use.

- ACCA – *Eminent Angel – pray reveal to us the glories of the eastern air.*

The mist clears. Now observe Acca's world for a short while. The vision fades. The mist returns.
We thank thee ACCA.

- NPAT [en-pe-at] – *Illustrious Angel - pray show us the eastern waters*

The mist clears. Now observe Npat's world for a short while. The vision fades. The mist returns.
We thank thee NPAT

- OTOI [o-toy] – *Distinguished Angel - pray show us the varied qualities of the earth of the East*

The mist clears. Now observe Otoi's world for a short while. The vision fades. The mist returns.
We thank thee OTOI

- PMOX [p-mox] – *Shining Angel- pray show us the secret properties of the eastern fire*

The mist clears. Now observe Pmox's world for a short while. The vision fades.
The mist returns.
We thank thee PMOX

Standing once again in front of the transparent door
Now thank the Angels before departing
AOVRRZ [a-o-ur-rez]
ALOAI [a-lo-ay]
Gods of the Fourth Angle Of The East, we thank thee and thy angels of the elements ACCA, NPAT, OTOI, PMOX for thy aid.
Pray depart in peace to thy abodes. May there ever be peace between us.
Amen

We now leave the World of the Elements of the East
Pass backwards through the Door into the Red Temple of the East.
The door closes, becomes solid, and the elemental signs fade therefrom.
Finally, thank the God of the Eastern quarter

ORO IBAH AOZPI
O Mighty God of the East, we thank thee for thy wisdom and guidance. Any understanding & knowledge gained of the elements of thy realm will be used for the good of all.
The temple walls begin to fade
ORO IBAH AOZPI
In thy name I declare the Temple of the Eastern Quarter closed.

Aire or Æthyr Workings

For the Aires imagine the walls, floor and ceiling of the Temple to be shimmering silvery white. Work facing East. Again the door to the Enochian realms is always ahead. Engraved on the silver door is the name of the Aire concerned in Latin and / or Enochian letters. The choice is up to the individual. Remember that Enochian reads from right to left:
TEX ⟨Enochian glyphs⟩
Commence the ritual by making the the Nineteenth Call or the *Call of the Æthyrs*, inserting the appropriate name and number of the Aire or Æthyr. Read it

first in English or one's first language and then in Enochian. In the spirit vision, move towards the door and cross the threshold into the Aire. Stand in a silvery mist.

Now request the presence of the Angelic Kings of the Aire by calling their names. TEX, the Thirtieth Aire, is used in the following example. Note that this Aire has four Angelic Kings unlike the other 29 which each have three.

ARFAOLG   [Ar- fa – oldg]
ZARNAAH   [Zar – na – ah]
HONONOL   [Ho -no – nol]
ZURCHOL   [Zu- re – kol]

O Angelic Kings of TEX pray guide us through thy realm and grant an insight into its mysteries

The mist clears. Commence the journey into the Aire noting all impressions, visions and sounds. Do not forget the name of the Aire or those of the Angelic Kings. Call upon them to halt drifting and to keep on the path. They give guidance and protect the traveller. In return treat them with respect and give thanks before leaving their domain. When it is felt the journey is complete, return to the transparent door the way you came.

The silvery mist returns. Stand with one's back to the door looking into the Aire or Æthyr.

Call the names of the Angelic Kings (in this case the four kings of TEX) and thank them for their aid.

ARFAOLG   [Ar- fa – oldg]
ZARNAAH   [Zar – na – ah]
HONONO   [(Ho -no – nol]
ZURCHOL   [Zu- re – kol]

We thank thee Angelic Kings of Tex, the Thirtieth Aire, for the safe transport through thy realm and the knowledge gained thereof. This we shall use beneficially for the earthly domain. Pray depart in peace to thy abodes. May there ever be peace between us.

Amen

Pass backwards through the doorway into the silvery Temple of the Aires.

The door closes and TEX fades there from. The temple walls become dim. Declare the Temple of the Aires closed.

Closing the door is a definitive act that effectively separates the magician from the Enochian world, so shut it firmly. Do not leave it swinging open, otherwise influences from that dimension could seep through uncontrolled into daily life.

Closing Ceremony

Once the doors to the Elemental worlds or to the Æthyrs have closed and their symbols faded away, it is time to bring the whole operation to a close.

1. See the temple of the Aires or the Quarter, in which one has been working, slowly grow faint and disappear. You are now back in your sacred space.

2. Perform the closing invocation

JEHOVAH TZABAOTH
In thy name and through these your 12 mystical names
ORO IBAH AOZPI, MOR DIAL HCTGA, MPH ARSL GAIOL, OIP TEAA PDOCE
The doors of all the temples are now closed and our journey complete.
JEHOVAH TZABAOTH
I thank thee, Amen.

3. Follow this with a general statement of closure or the Licence to Depart.

The ALPHA and the OMEGA, the beginning and the end, in the spirit of AZOTH. I thank thee, O Mighty Ones, for thy aid. All wisdom gained will be used beneficially and for the good.

If any spirits or forces are entrapped in this place, pray depart ye in peace to thy abodes.

May there ever be peace between us. I thank thee.
Amen

4. Now perform the Closing Sign or the Closing of the Veil

- Stand with both arms outstretched before you in line with the shoulders with the palms of the hands vertical and facing inwards.
- Slowly bring the arms together until the palms meet, as if drawing curtains across a window.

5. Qabalistic Cross
6. Record all details of the working.

The foregoing chapter has been mainly concerned with creating a sacred space in which to work and the build-up of a visionary Enochian temple, as well as providing a guide to the rituals. Full details of the complete rituals for both the Æthyrs and the Elements of the Four Quarters feature in Chapter Eleven.

A Note on Enochian Sex Magick

Although there is occasional erotic content present in a few of the visions, sex magick was not employed as an aid for the pathworking rituals recorded below. Both Aleister Crowley and David Shoemaker make use of this in their ritual work. The sex between Crowley and Victor Neuberg, when scrying the Fourteenth Æthyr on the summit of Da'leh Addin, a small mountain near Bou Saâda, is well documented. Shoemaker uses sex or "Eroto-Comotose Lucidity" (as he terms it) for scrying the Eighth Æthyr. The process is described in detail in *The Winds of Wisdom*.[51] The male "Adept"[52] reclines on a mattress to the west of the altar with a variety of sex toys and "appropriate intoxicants" close at hand. He is blindfolded, masturbated and variously stimulated by gender non-specific "assistants" for up to three and a half hours, at one point reciting the Governors' Names and "rising to a great height".

However, neither Crowley nor Shoemaker's resultant visions are any more exotic or extravagant than their other visions, but this may not be the same for everyone. It is, therefore, entirely up to the individual whether to use sex magick as an aid to scrying. The only downside to Shoemaker's ritual is having to clean up afterwards, so it may be an idea to place a disposable protective cover over the mattress.

A more balanced view of Enochian sex magick is provided by Lon Milo DuQuette in *Enochian World of Aleister Crowley* (1991). The book includes not only the complete text and a valuable commentary on Crowley's *Liber Chanockh Sub Figurâ LXXXIV*,[53] but also offers "practical instructions concerning powerful sexual applications of the system", which are described in a contributory article, *Techniques of Enochian Sex Magick*, by Tantric practitioner Christopher S. Hyatt in Chapter Seven of that work. The operation is designed for two participants, the

---

51. See pages 92-95 of that work..
52. Shoemaker acknowledges that the process would have to be adapted for a female adept, but gives no details.

Magician and the Assistant, but it can be adapted to suit solo workings.
Gender is irrelevant, but the roles must be agreed beforehand and the decision adhered to throughout the working. Sincerity is important and Dr Hyatt issues a strong warning against abusing the system.

"*There must be no ambiguity about the willingness of either participant to take part in an operation of this kind. If one participant has to be coerced, begged or tricked into participation, the vortex of ill-will that will emanate from the offended party will insure not only the failure of the operation but also the destruction of a more precious 'magical asset', the respect of another human being*". (p.118)

Following on from this, the next section examines the necessity of safety in ritual.

Magical Health and Safety

1. Disclaimer: The preceding guide is one possible way of working with the Æthyrs and the Great Table. It is offered as a means to access part of Dee and Kelley's angelic or Enochian system and is not intended to be followed to the letter or even accepted. If appealing, it can be adjusted to suit individual requirements. Select areas to study rather than attempt all.

2. Do not work with Enochian if there exists the slightest doubt and there is not total commitment. Proceed slowly, setting a suitable pace at which to work. Even if the process may prove lengthy, it is still not wise to rush. Do not be hurried by others.

3. Make sure all the working areas are ritually cleansed; for example, always perform banishing rituals or an opening prayer or conjuration, even if simply meditating on an angelic or a divine name.

4. Afterwards, ensure the temple or working area is properly closed down. At the very least, perform the Qabalistic Cross to complete the ritual cycle, making sure to thank all forces, spirits, gods and angels for their help and guidance. Remember the maxim: *They guide and protect, so treat with respect.*

If after dismissal, one still feels in an altered state and that forces remain, simply perform the closing ceremony again. It is better to be safe than sorry.

---

53. Also known as *Liber Chanokh Sub Figurâ LXXXIV: A Brief Abstract of the Symbolic Representation of the Universe derived by Dr John Dee through the scrying of Edward Kelly*, the booklet succinctly explains the main features of the Enochian system as practised by the Golden Dawn. "Chanockh" is an early form of "Enoch". For more information on this work, see Appendix I.

5. After the final ceremonies, record all details of the working. This also helps to bring one "back to earth". If possible, make jottings or rough notes during the ritual to aid the memory.

6. Be sincere. Do not use any knowledge or insights gained for selfish ends, as Enochian seems to have a "sorting out" and karmic effect.

7. Do not expect instant results. Put the working to the back of the mind and forget about it. Avoid becoming anxious for a result, as this will only inhibit progress. An awareness of the outcome of the operation will become apparent when the time is right. Individual circumstances will govern how long this will be.

By keeping these points in mind, encountering malignant forces, such as Choronzon[54] in ZAX the Tenth Æthyr, should present no problem, if indeed they manifest at all. Choronzon's presence in ZAX rests upon the concept that the Aires correspond to the Tree of Life with three Aires being assigned to each of the ten Sephiroth. Kelley felt Choronzon, "that mighty devil", was the Arch Fiend who caused the Fall from Paradise by the tempting of Eve. This act symbolises the quest of the Spirit to seek knowledge of physical manifestation. The experience is represented by the ghostly sephira of Daath or Knowledge, which is centred in The Abyss between Gedulah or Chesed, the last sephira of the Formative World of Yetzirah, and the Spiritual Triad of Kether, Chokmah and Binah. If the Aires relate to the Tree of Life, then Aires 12, 11 and 10 will equate with Gedulah and 9, 8 and 7 to Binah with the Abyss and the demon Choronzon, "the Dweller in the Abyss", lurking between Aires 10 and 9. He is not really an individual. As Crowley explains:

"The Abyss is empty of being; it is filled with all possible forms, each equally inane, each therefore evil in the only true sense of the word – that is, meaningless but malignant, insofar as it craves to become real. These forms swirl senselessly into haphazard heaps like dust devils, and each such chance aggregation asserts itself to be an individual, and shrieks,"I am I!"though aware all the time that its elements have no true bond, so that the slightest disturbance dissipates the delusion." [55]

In the Tenth Aire Crowley stood on the very brink of The Abyss. It is at this point, where the knowledge of the physical world must be relinquished; where the Glories of the Earth must be forsaken; and where the totality of one's existence

---

54. Dee spells this as "Coronzom" in his diary. However, the form "Choronzon" will be retained in relation to Crowley's dealings with the demon. See Appendix I for further information
55. Crowley, *The Vision and the Voice* (1998), p.24.

must be confronted, accepting both good and evil. The experience will be peculiar to the individual. For Crowley, it would seem that nothing short of the Devil himself could personify the sum-total of his "knowledge". The old life vanishes and there is rebirth to a higher order. When the time is right the "Fiend" will be passed by. In order to successfully cross The Abyss, the magician "must rid himself of every trace of impurity, for above the Abyss all opposites are included in a single idea."[56] Absolutely no trace of the ego can remain; the personal self must be annihilated. Failure would enslave the magician to the demon, "corrupting every subsequent undertaking and bringing disaster in its wake".[57] This may seem overly dramatic, but on a practical level, it will represent a cleansing and purification or a smoothing out of previous difficulties - provided they are admitted to, of course. The experience will be completely individualistic. It may be imperceptible with realisation dawning later, creating a fresh slate from which to progress. Only then can one finally cry:

"Begone Choronzon!"

56. Ibid, p.22.
57. For further information, see "Aleister Crowley in the Desert" in *The Place of Enchantment: British Occultism and the Culture of the Modern* by Alex Owen, (Chicago: University of Chicago Press, 2004), pp. 186-202.

CHAPTER SIX

THE ÆTHYRS, QABALAH AND CORRESPONDENCES

Aligning the Aires or Æthyrs with the Tree of Life as described in the previous chapter may possibly help to explain Crowley's tussle with "that Mighty devil" Choronzon / Coronzom, but the technique of assigning three Æthyrs to each sephiroth (four in the case of Malkuth) is somewhat arbitrary and it has led to the process being questioned by some Enochian scholars. The issue is complicated by the spiritual realms of the Four Worlds or stages through which the divine light or energy forever flows on its journey from the Unmanifest to materialisation.

In the descending chain of Existence, each of the four Worlds has an associated element and a letter of the Tetragrammaton or the Hebrew Four-Letter Name of God, IHVH – יהוה. They are listed below. The section of the Tree of Life and its constituent sephiroth to which each World corresponds is also indicated.

1. **ATZILUTH** – the World of Archetypes or Emanation; the World of Spirit; Divine Consciousness.
   KETHER
   FIRE
   י YOD – the first letter of the Name of God

2. **BRIAH** – the World of Creation; the World of the Soul; Archangelic Consciousness.
   CHOKMAH, BINAH
   WATER
   ה HEH – the second letter of the Name of God

3. **YETZIRAH** – the World of Formation; the Mental World; the Realm of the Angelic Orders; Angelic Consciousness
CHESED, GEBURAH, TIPHARETH, NETZACH, HOD, YESOD
AIR
ו VAU – the third letter of the Name of God.

4. **ASSIAH** – the World of Matter or Action; Material Manifestation; Elemental Consciousness.
MALKUTH
EARTH
ה HEH – the fourth letter of the Name of God

Sometimes a fifth world is added. This is actually a prior stage, referred to as Adam Kadmon or the Primordial Man, which is the very first pure emanation from which the ten divine emanations of the sephiroth of Atziluth proceed. This world is the essence or a blueprint of the ten sephiroth before their emanation from Kether, the first sephira of the Tree of Life. Everything originates in the so-called Veils of Negative Existence which precede manifestation down through the Four Worlds. These preliminary stages or veils are three in number, commencing with a state of complete non-existence, the Unmanifest, "No-Thing" or nothingness, called *Ain* in Hebrew. A contraction occurs within the nothingness resulting in a state of Limitlessness or Divine Infinity, basically an ocean of negative light, called *Ain Soph*. This movement produces the third state, an awareness, or a sensing of its own existence, which is referred to as Enlightened Limitlessness or Infinite Light known as *Ain Soph Aur*. It is from this that the first emanations of creation arise forming a blueprint for the sephiroth in Adam Kadmon. The emanations constitute ten aspects or variations of the divine light from which the sephiroth are formed.

The passage of the divine light through the Four Worlds and their associated elements to concretion in Assiah brings to mind the Angel Nalvage's description of the Aires on 21 May 1584:

> "Understand, therefore, that from the fire to the earth, there are 30 places or abidings: one above and beneath another". [58]

This could imply that the Thirty Aires incorporate the Four Worlds. Each world contains its own Tree of Life, as do all the individual component sephiroth. The

---

58. *T&FR*, p.140.

trees are quite separate, but overlap. The Kether of one Tree will coincide with the Malkuth of the Tree in the next World above. This overlapping also applies to all the trees in the individual sephiroth.

Added to the process is the simultaneous development of the human soul through five dimensions of awareness:

1. YECHIDAH – the divine or collective essence of the soul; unity with God; an undifferentiated quintessence.
2. CHAYAH – the everlasting soul; spiritual awareness.
3. NESHEMAH – the spiritual or sacred soul, providing divine intellect and an awareness of the self.
4. RUACH – the mental soul, including emotions, morality and rationality.
5. NEPHESH – the animal or vegetative soul, including natural instincts and cravings.

Again, as with the Four Worlds, each one of these stages also includes all the others.

To deal with this complexity any further is outside the scope of this work. Some writers, including David Shoemaker and Pat Zalewski, have incorporated parts of the Four Worlds into the Thirty Æthyrs by relating the ten sephiroth of Yetzirah to Aires 30 to 21, Aires 20 to 11 to those of Briah, and Aires 10 to 1 to Atziluth. However, this arrangement creates more questions than it answers. It should be noted that this perspective only relates to levels of Assiah and not the creation process as a whole. It also effectively rules out Aleister Crowley negotiating the Abyss in ZAX, the Tenth Aire. Located between Chesed and Binah, the Abyss would now be encountered between PAZ and ZOM, the Fourth and Third Aires, with Choronzon/Coronzom possibly making an appearance when scrying PAZ.

The present study has treated the Aires as the heavens immediately surrounding the Earth, mainly because of their direct relation to the Great Table of Earth, which contains the names of all the gods and angels of the Four Quarters and the Four Elements. A variant reading of the letters on the Great Table produces the spiritual names (sometimes called "Governors"), along with their sigils, of the Ninety-One Parts of the Earth, upon which the Æthyrs can bring influence to bear. In theory, entering a region on a spiritual or astral level will bring foresight of future events and, by working positive magic, beneficial changes can be wrought in troubled lands. The angels of the Aires "would bring in and again dispose Kings and all Governments upon Earth, and vary the Natures of things: with variation of every moment". [59]

By accepting the whole action takes place within the World of Assiah, arranging the Aires on the Tree of Life by the simple method of three Æthyrs per sephira enables the magician to employ the system of Qabalistic correspondences in order to enhance and increase the effectiveness of the rituals with the aid of appropriate symbols and associations, such as incenses, colours and various items of magical equipment within the temple or place of working. As Stephen Skinner explains in his *The Complete Magician's Tables* (2006):

> "*Magic is based on correspondences. Magic most powerfully uses them when they are put together in a well constructed ritual. The denizens of other worlds and other spaces do not always speak our language, but they do respond to correctly assembled rituals where the colours, perfumes, gestures and words of power are all attuned to the same wavelength. The whole science of magic, before the advent of universal literacy, was based on correspondences. … Knowledge of these correspondences can help us understand the structure of thought, and the nature of memory, as well as the techniques of magic. These correspondences can even be used to alter this reality, not to just describe it.*"[60]

Some of the correspondences are centuries old and can be found in the 13th century grimoire, *Liber Juratis* or *The Sworn Book of Honorius*, as well as in the writings of Albertus Magnus (c. 1193 – 1280) and Heinrich Cornelius Agrippa von Nettesheim (1486 – 1535). The latter's influential *Three Books of Occult Philosophy* was written in 1510 and circulated in manuscript copies until it was published in the early 1530s in Cologne. Many more correspondences originate from the work of the Hermetic Order of the Golden Dawn during the 1890s and the early years of the twentieth century. Aleister Crowley listed and tabulated these in his book *Liber777*, which was first published in 1909. Recently, this system of tabulation was expanded in considerable detail with over four times as many tables by Stephen Skinner in the aforementioned *The Complete Magician's Tables* to which, along with *Liber777*, the interested reader is directed. However, it must be borne in mind that some of the later correspondences could derive from these authors' own

---

59. *T&FR*, p.140.
60. Stephen Skinner. *The Complete Magician's Tables* (Singapore: Golden Hoard Press, 2006), p.13.

personal experiences and may not be suitable for everybody. Ultimately, it is up to individuals to decide for themselves which correspondences are the most effective and even source their own if necessary.

To conclude, a limited selection of correspondences tying together the Aires, the Sephiroth and various esoteric attributions are offered as an example. To include more has the danger of implanting suggestions, which could result in visions that are too subjective. The sephirotic correspondences apply to all three Aires located within a particular sephira. Each of the Four Worlds has its own scale of colours for the sephiroth of its Tree of Life. The colour scale for the Creative World of Briah, also known as the Queen Scale, is listed here. It represents the first positive appearance of colour and, as such, is considered the most effective for use in meditation and ritual workings.

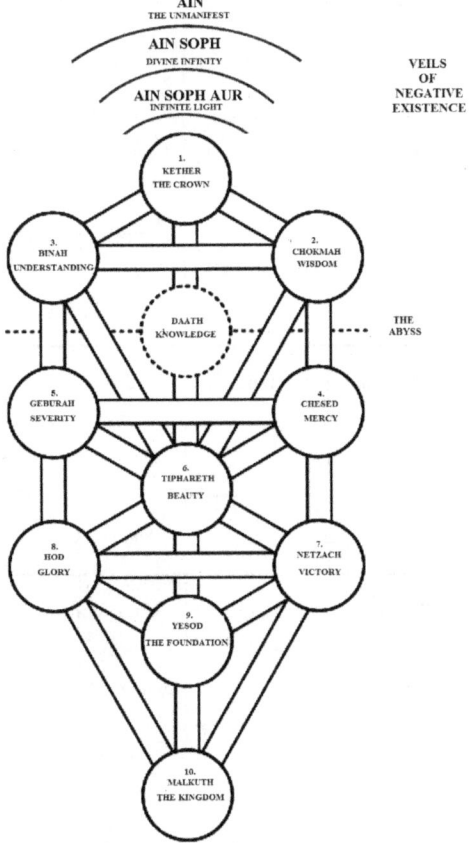

13. Qabalistic Tree Of Life (© R.E. Cousins)

A SELECTION OF CORRESPONDENCES

ÆTHYR	SEPHIRA & MUNDANE CHAKRA	COLOUR Briatic Scale	PERFUMES & PLANTS	GEMSTONES	METALS & MINERALS
1. LIL	1. KETHER	Pure White Brilliance	Ambergris	Diamond	Aurum Potabile
2. ARN	Primum Mobile First Swirlings		Almond in flower		(Drinkable Gold) [61]
3. ZOM					
4. PAZ	2. CHOKMAH	Grey	Musk	Star Ruby	Phosphorus
5. LIT	The Zodiac		Amaranth [62]	Turquoise	
6. MAZ					
7. DEO	2. BINAH	Black	Civet, Myrrh	Pearl, Onyx	Lead
8. ZID	Saturn		Cypress, Yew	Star Sapphire	
9. ZIP			Opium Poppy		
10. ZAX	4. CHESED	Blue	Cedar	Amethyst, Lapis Lazuli	Tin
11. ICH	Jupiter		Olive, Oak	Sapphire	
12. LOE			Shamrock		
13. ZIM	5. GEBURAH	Scarlet Red	Cinnamon	Ruby	Iron
14. VTA	Mars		Dragons Blood		Sulphur
15. OXO			Nettle, Nux Vomica		

61. The gold essence, Aurum Potabile, is the drinkable gold of the alchemists. It is the legendary Elixir of Life, said to cure all ills and grant eternal life   62. Common Name: *Love-Lies-Bleeding*

A SELECTION OF CORRESPONDENCES

ÆTHYR	SEPHIRA & MUNDANE CHAKRA	COLOUR Briatic Scale	PERFUMES & PLANTS	GEMSTONES	METALS & MINERALS
16. LEA	6. TIPHARETH	Yellow (Gold)	Olibanum	Topaz, Yellow Diamond	Gold
17. TAN	Sol (The Sun)		Frankincense		
18. ZEN			Sunflower, Bay		
19. POP	7. NETZACH	Emerald Green	Red Sandalwood	Emerald	Copper
20. CHR	Venus		Benzoin, Rose		Arsenic
21. ASP			Rose (plant)		
22. LIN	8. HOD	Orange	Storax	Fire Opal	Mercury
23. TOR	Mercury		Alchemilla Mollis (Moly)[63]		(Quicksilver)
24. NIA					
25. VTI	9. YESOD	Violet	Jasmine	Quartz, Pearl	Silver
26. DES	Luna (The Moon)		White Sandalwood	Moonstone	
27. ZAA			Mandrake		
28. BAG	10. MALKUTH	Citrine, Olive Russet, Black	Dittany of Crete	Rock Crystal	Magnesium Sulphate[64]
29. RII	The Four Elements		Lily, Ivy		
30. TEX			Willow		

63. Common Name: *Lady's Mantle*   64. Epsom salt

PART TWO

AN ENOCHIAN TRAVELOGUE

PREAMBLE

As mentioned in the Introduction the following visionary journeys were recorded by the author over a period of twenty-three years between 1995 and 2018. Originally there were four participants who scryed the elemental worlds and the first few Æthyrs together, before the group disbanded after completing the Twenty-Sixth Aire in 1996.

The methodology of scrying the Thirty Æthyrs is summarised in the following quotation by Lon Milo DuQuette, and the principles are the same for the spiritual exploration of the Four Elements of the terrestrial world.

> 'The Thirty Æthyrs are the "heavens" or Aires of the [Enochian] system. Starting with the 30th Æthyr and working to the 1st, the magician explores only as far as his or her personal level of Initiation will permit. The process is comparable to "pathworkings" of the Qabalistic system. In Enochian terms, the "Great Work" of the magician is to master all 30 Æthyrs (starting with 30 and ending with 1).
>
> Experiences with the 30 Æthyrs are highly personal and entirely unique to each magician. Working with the Æthyrs can be a lifetime endeavour and it is entirely presumptuous and inappropriate for another individual to "guide" another in this area.' [65]

---

65. Lon Milo DuQuette. *Enochian World of Aleister Crowley* (1991), p. 29.

CHAPTER SEVEN

THE ELEMENTAL WORLDS OF THE FOUR QUARTERS

The journey began with four participants exploring the elemental worlds of the Four Quarters. In these early sessions we were still "finding our feet". Over time, the rituals were gradually refined and the visions improved as a consequence. Although our experiences were discussed at the time, only the visions of the author feature here, as the other records have not survived. The results must be considered as "first steps" and as such consist of descriptions of various terrains and elementary observations free from complex analyses. A later and more in-depth exploration of the elemental worlds and TEX, the Thirtieth Aire, was undertaken by a group of six scryers at the Atlantis Bookshop in London in 2008, which is subject of Chapter Eleven.

The Quarters or Watchtowers were scryed clockwise through the cardinal points, namely: East, South, West and North; while the Elements of each quarter were explored in the order given in Dee's diaries, that is: Air, Water, Earth and Fire. The original note form of some entries has been retained.

THE EASTERN QUARTER
AIR

A windswept landscape; the wind roars and circles around me in a clockwise direction. Gold sparks are in the air. All the dross is blown away in a hurricane along with all tiresome problems.

WATER
Watery imagery – floods, waterfalls. The water flows clockwise, full of golden drops of purity which washes all and runs clear over the feet.

EARTH
An airey landscape of calm and peace; pastel colours. I stand on high ground looking down on the world. A sense of freedom and the essence of new beginnings as trees send out new shoots from their branches.

FIRE
Bathed in fire – a calming balm; relaxed and peaceful atmosphere. Fire is needed to purify and consecrate. There is a wall of flame before me. Fierce at first, but becomes gentle, peaceful and inspirational. Feel the very strong presence of PMOX, the Angel of the Fire of the Eastern Quarter. The intent to explore the elemental worlds is reassured. The fire of the spirit within is stirred. I feel renewed.

By Winn's Common, South East London
Monday, 30 January 1995, 8:30 p.m.

THE WESTERN QUARTER
With opening invocations I experience a tremendous shift in levels of consciousness. I sense the unfolding of the petals of a flower, after which I seem to whirl off to the quarter.

AIR
I float amongst calm, white clouds seeing valleys and hills below. Hills are ancient, smooth and glaciated.

WATER
Green water runs over my feet, and then great aquamarine waves wash over me, cleansing me to a white brightness.

EARTH
I am again amongst the white clouds, but I am unable to see any ground below. Feeling unsteady, I drift higher in the sky. I call RNIL, the Angel of the Earth of the Western Quarter to take me back to the door of the temple. Felt my physical form weakening.

FIRE

I have feelings of cold and warmth simultaneously; a sensation of a spiralling movement within me, possibly spiritual fire.

Overall, this is a very watery quarter. The other scryers had similar experiences revealing flow, flexibility, and non-rigidity.

By Winn's Common, South East London
Thursday, 2 March 1995, approx. 8:30 p.m.

THE SOUTHERN QUARTER
AIR

Seemingly an infinite dark black pit, the essence of the earth, exists underneath actual existence. It is of endless depth. Then an upward spiralling or revolving occurred. Lights flickered within the vortex. These lights aerate the Earth to stimulate growth. I call MSAL, the Angel of Air of the Southern Quarter, to steady myself.

WATER

A whiteness, but rivulets of water are running and rushing in all directions throughout, nourishing the earth forever, creating growth. It becomes mesmeric after a while. I call on IABA, the Water Angel of the South in order to stop drifting, and again to stop a repetitive ditty raging through the head describing the continuous, nurturing operation of the water:

Here, there and everywhere,
Up and down, all around
Ever and forever.

EARTH

I am suspended among white clouds far above the Earth with its hills, woods and villages -

"The fruits of the Element of Earth". I have a surreal and overwhelming desire to touch the Earth with a toe; a desire to touch manifestation and experience this for one fleeting moment. May be this is an awakening to commence the process of growth.

FIRE
Darkness reigns but there is a suggestion of light, fire and spirit present in the depths – an energy within. I am the kernel of a seed in the earth (the spirit of life within the earth, and within the seed) - an innocent being which will grow from the nourishment of the other quarters of the Great Table.

By Winn's Common, South East London
Monday, 10 April 1995, 7:30 p.m.

THE NORTHERN QUARTER
AIR
Before me is a roaring wall of flame, fanned by air streams. Gold specks are within the flames, which cool, cleanse and consecrate, thereby ensuring the removal of all impurities.

WATER
Water laps my feet. Little golden flames are on the surface. I become a rarefied being of pure crystal, floating in the clear water.

EARTH
Dark caves illuminated by myriads of flames and fires. Here is the Spirit of Earth that is the essence of existence and its development – the spirit of growth. I dance down tunnels, leaping with joy in sublime ecstasy. Suddenly, I burst forth into the light. Layers seemed to peel away from my form. It was like the growth of a seed. This spirit – the fire within the earth – is there forever. It is the essence of the Northern Angle.

FIRE
Absolute blackness; I am unaware of my body. I step into the darkness and sense a movement or an initial swirling in the Blackness. However, I did not become one with this motion, a realisation which would have allowed development. This movement continues seemingly indefinitely and I realise it had to be terminated in order to return to the temple. Instantly, I feel myself to be swirling clouds, gradually gaining density until my body reformulates at the threshold of the temple, ready to return.

When recording the experiences after the mediation, I felt secure and safe within the circle or place of working. Towards the end of the ceremony, I caught a glimpse of brilliance in the crystal, which was placed on a plan of the watchtowers in the centre of the circle.

To consolidate this final elemental ceremony, Kelley's *Vision of the Four Castles* (see Chapter Two) was recited after closing the Temple of the North.

By Winn's Common, South East London
Wednesday, 31 May 1995, 7:40 p.m.

CHAPTER EIGHT

THE AIRES FROM THE THIRTIETH (TEX) TO THE TWENTY-FIRST (ASP)

The Thirthieth Æthyr TEX
Angelic Kings ARFAOLG • ZARNAAH • HONONOL • ZURCHOL

The *Call of the Æthyrs* was very powerful. I am floating in white clouds above the elemental, cubical world of the Four Watchtowers. I have an overwhelming sense of freedom – a freedom from the shackles of the material world. I am aware the Earth was beneath me, but I no longer cared. I had no need of it. No longer is there a worry of earthly things.

I begin to move clockwise through the beautiful realm. A white landscape, a white sky with imperceptible stars - is this the etheric world encircling and co-existing with the elemental world?

An extreme peacefulness pervades all. Looking up, I have the impression of the endless realms of the Æthyrs above and beyond me. My form seems to dissolve and I become one with the stars – a star being. I sense the presence of The Sphinx. It is the all-seeing eye. It contains the knowledge of the secrets of the Universe.

At this point, the circling motion slows and the atmosphere becomes denser until a mist forms signalling it is time to return.

A new age has begun; a new journey. The material or elemental worlds below are no longer an attraction. I believe this is the successful beginning of the journey through the Æthyrs. The other participants felt similarly.

The Call of the Æthyrs demands the forsaking of the terrestrial world and this reinforced our visions.

"And the dwelling places, Let them forget their names:"

The work of Man, and his pomp, Let them be defaced.

His buyldings, let them become Caves for the beasts of the field."

> By Winn's Common, South East London
> Wednesday, 25 October 1995, approx. 7:45 p.m.

Note

As the opening ceremony requires all participants to be standing, it proved advisable to adopt a seated position for the pathworking immediately after the Call and before entering the Aire. The meditation could then proceed in comfort from the start and avoid the interruption of later physical manoeuvres.

THE Twenty-ninth Æthyr RII ᛭᛭ᛠ
Angelic Kings HONONOL • ZARNAAH • ARFAOLG

The whole Aire seems to be whirling clockwise. Wind is whistling. I have a sensation of weightlessness. I am floating and at the same time slowly rising to higher planes.

Matter is far below; pulsating, brilliant heavens are above. I am amidst white swirling clouds, pure beauty and simplicity. These are not the same as the mist one encounters when first entering the Aire.

Now I see web-like structures of white-interweaving strands. They are holding together the etheric Thirtieth Aire or TEX. This is the cohesion of TEX. It is the inner structure of the Aire and it binds the demesnes of the four elements into the unity, which is our terrestrial world.

The interdependence of the Twenty-Ninth and Thirtieth Aires (RII and TEX) is reflected in the fact that three of the four Angelic Kings of TEX, namely: HONONOL , ZARNAAH and ARFAOLG, are also the three Angelic Kings of RII.

> By Winn's Common, South East London
> Sunday, 11 February 1996, approx. 3:00 p.m.

The Twenty-eighth Æthyr BAG ⌐⚡⚡P
Angelic Kings • LAVAVOT • ZARZILG • ZURCHOL

Temple was purified with water and consecrated with fire before proceeding with the full ritual. The build-up of the temple was very vivid. I vibrate BAG three times upon entering the Aire and greet the Angelic Kings. There are billowing clouds as I stand in the Æthyr. The Sun, when not obscured by clouds, is brilliant, but despite this the temperature remains pleasantly cool.

The Earth seems primordial. I am of great stature. I turn to the right and start to move through the Aire. I feel this Æthyr to be a base-line on which to build spirituality. I feel free of earthly desires, needs and longings. Roads to spiritual development stretch ahead. It is up to the individual to choose their path.

The system demands purity of intent and does not suffer the greedy and insincere.

By Winn's Common, South East London
Saturday, 2 March 1996, approx. 2:30 p.m.

Note
The last statement is an indication that there is dissention forming within the group

The Twenty-seventh ÆTHYR ZAA ⚡⚡P
Angelic Kings • ZIRACAH • ZARNAAH • GEBABAL

The sky is pale blue. I am in a forest of bare, leafless trees on the side of a mountain. A ground mist swirls around my feet. I climb onto a rocky platform. The Sun is above me and I take off and fly towards it.

Everything is illuminated in a golden light. The shadows are long. I travel towards an ornate temple in the mountains. It is the palace of the Angelic Kings of ZAA. Inside, light streams through enormous windows stretching from the floor to the ceiling. Before me, the three Angelic Kings sit on their thrones. I bow to the Kings, who say,

"Welcome to our realm of the Twenty-seventh Aire. You are infused with the Sun ready for your wondrous journey. This is a realm above the clouds. It enriches the Soul."

I go down on my knees and the Kings continue,

"Take these gifts to remind you of your holiness."

ZIRACAH gives me a pale blue crystal containing a flower within its depths.

ZARNAAH presents a jewelled orb

GEBABAL hands me a little gold casket in the form of a castle with four corner towers.

They are assembled by putting the crystal inside the casket and placing the orb on top.

"Arise; this shall be your guide. Consult when in difficulty by gazing into the blue stone."

I wrap my gift in a blue silk cloth. I leave it on a pedestal in a niche next to the door to the Temple of the Aires as I return.

By Winn's Common, South East London
Sunday, 10 March 1996, 2:40 p.m.

14. Sketch of the casket made during the meditation

The Twenty-sixth Æthyr   DES ⟨sigil⟩
Angelic Kings • ARFAOLG • CADAAMP • ARFAOLG

Upon entering the Aire, I collect the casket with the blue crystal and the orb from the pedestal in the niche by the door.

I hear the beating of wings. Blackbirds are flying above, circling clockwise.

A white horse arrives. I mount the animal and gallop away, but leave the casket behind.

From the top of a hill, I survey a cold land, bathed in a multicoloured sunset of whites, blues, pinks, mauves and purples. I travel on until nightfall, when I arrive at the Palace of the Angelic Kings. A pale moon shines above.

I enter a vast burnished hall. The three kings sit on their thrones at the far end. ARFAOLG has a dual role in this Aire. He appears as twins, continually shifting between the first and third throne in split second flicks, creating the illusion of being on both thrones simultaneously.

I believe the casket is a key to the Aire and the door back into the Enochian Temple again, which is the reason I left it at the door of the Aire. It can now act as a beacon to guide my return. This use is confirmed by the Kings.

Suddenly, an enormous arc of golden light appears behind them. They arise from their thrones and walk towards the ray. They are wearing deep purple robes with gold and silver sigils. They invite me to stand in the light. I become a gold being. My body is bathed, purified and infused with the golden light. I am now worthy to make my journey through the Aires. As I return from the light, the Kings throw over me a plain purple cloak. There are no occult sigils adorning the robe but the silver clasp bore this sign.*

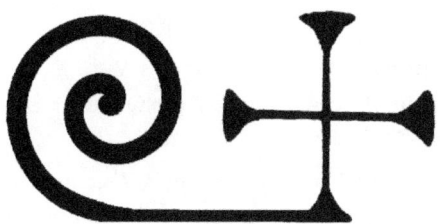

15. Sign of DES, the Twenty-Sixth Æthyr

The cloak is to be worn on future journeys and hung on the Aire side of the door to the Enochian Temple. In this way, no-one enters the Aire wearing it and always returns to the temple disrobed. Putting on the cloak indicates a step forward on the spiritual road and indicates that one is ready to rise to a higher level. The colour purple signifies, that it is a journey involving wisdom, creativity, a superior dignity and, ultimately, triumph. The cloak infuses the wearer with knowledge from earlier experiences and, at the same time, offers protection from malign influences and earlier unfortunate events which could still affect the future. [66]

•The sign is the plan of creation. From the spiral of the first swirlings of the Universe, the world of matter eventually materialises, represented here as the equal-armed cross or the Cross of the Elements.

By Winn's Common, South East London
Saturday, 16 March 1996, 2:55 p.m.

Note

Following the working with DES, the Twenty-Sixth Aire on the 16th March, it was decided by all participants to close down the group and pursue our own individual paths. I decided to carry on with the journey through the Æthyrs. However, before doing so, I felt it was essential to purify the Egregore or the collective mind of the group of all harmful influences. The group mind is an aggregate formed from the experiences, thoughts, and emotions, both good and bad, of all the participants during the workings. Any negativity is destructive and draining for the Egregore and the participants. The aim of the cleansing is to consign all malignancy to the past, thereby enabling me to continue my travels afresh, no longer hampered by the old Egregore.

CEREMONY TO CLEANSE THE EGREGORE

After the preliminary opening ceremonies were performed, I entered the Enochian Temple of the Æthyrs and the Four Quarters and made the following proclamation:

"*There are persons and forces within this temple that are no longer welcome. They have abandoned their work for the lure of earthly power. BAG, the Twenty-Eighth Æthyr, instructs the need for purity of intent. The insincere are not tolerated. In their*

---

66. The use of the robe as a Cloak of Knowledge is described in CHR, the Twentieth Æthyr.

pursuit of material gain, they have endeavoured to secure these workings for themselves — even though they failed to understand their import. They took little interest other than how they could employ the worldly status of the description "Angelic or Enochian Magic" for personal gain. They ignored their promise to use any knowledge gained selflessly for the good of all. It is felt that they are unworthy to remain as part of the Egregore and be allowed admission to the Enochian Temple of the Æthyrs and the Four Quarters.

> Following this, I visualised myself in the Temple of the Aires
> YEHOVAH!
> ADONAI HA ARETZ!
> In Thy Twelve Mystical Names of God
> ORO IBAH AOZPI
> MOR DIAL HCTGA
> MPH ARSL GAIOL (GAI-OL)
> OIP TEAA PDOCE

I dismiss you [Names] from the Enochian Temple of the Æthyrs until such time that wisdom permits your return. I turn around and with arms outstretched walk towards them with the power until they leave the temple.

The temple fades and I now visualise myself in the Temple of the Four Quarters.
> YEHOVAH!
> ADONAI HA ARETZ!

In Thy Twelve Mystical Names of God (repeat as above), I banish you [Names] from the Temple of the Four Quarters in which you shall never set foot again until such time when wisdom permits a return.

You will no longer understand the mysteries of the Angelic Tablets. All knowledge gained is now forgotten and all procedures have faded from your memories.

> Turn to the East

In the name of ORO IBAH AOZPI, I banish you from the Eastern Quarter.
> Turn to the South

In the name of MOR DIAL HCTGA, I banish you from the Southern Quarter.
> Turn to the West

In the name of MPH ARSL GAIOL (GAI-OL), I banish you from the Western Quarter.
Turn to the North
In the name of OIP TEAA PDOCE, I banish you from the Northern Quarter.
BEGONE!

Everything fades
I declare the Egregore purified and the Temples cleansed and free from the unwelcome presence.
The usual closing ceremonies followed.

By Epping Forest, North East London
Saturday, 27April 1996, 4:55 p.m.

Note
In LEA, the Sixteenth Æthyr, the banished members were able to return, but by then they were no longer particularly interested in Enochian magic and were happily pursing their own individual paths, which maybe the Enochian studies had helped them to discover.

The Twenty-fifth Æthyr VTI LEA
Angelic Kings • ZARNAAH • ZIRACAH • ARFAOLG

FIRST VISION
Immediately after Cleansing the Egregore, I enter VTI the Twenty-Fifth Aire. The Kings ask, *"Are you alone?"* I reply in the affirmative and a robed figure leads me away. It is extremely hot and I have visions of creatures crawling from the depths. They are similar to those in a Hieronymus Bosch painting. I drift, experiencing shape-shifting scenes.

I have not moved from the door. There are many visions. I run and play on pure white beaches; then I am on a bridge in a silvery atmosphere. Strange sounds rend the air.

I need to order this chaos. Friendly people come and fade away all the time. I am now in a tenement block beside the sea.

I awake from a sleep, feeling refreshed. I realise I am wearing the purple cloak. It is my protection from the visionary onslaught.

Suddenly, the visual jumble vanishes . I start walking the circuit of the Aire. I am in a concrete corridor. I feel free from all dangerous elements.

A voice says, *"You have done well."*

I see a barque on the sea. It is vessel of the Sun God. I am bathed in the light of the Sun. I feel purified from all material detritus. I am again a golden being. The Æthyrs stretch above me, brighter than I have ever seen. I feel I have passed on from the darkness of before.

By Epping Forest, North East London
Saturday, 27April 1996, 6:00 p.m.

SECOND VISION

I return to VTI for a second visit, in order to be sure that I am completely free of all the mire, so that I can enjoy untainted experiences.

I put on the cloak, leaving the casket and its stone on the pedestal by the door. The air is pure and I feel light-headed as I pass through the Æthyr. Hills covered in flowers surround me, but the sky is grey.

This is a foundation for the next stage of the journey. The confusion of the first visit has gone. I kneel and the Kings place a gold crown on my head.* I am completely surprised.

I have been pulled through the darkness to the threshold of glory and victory. [67] I am ready.

* The crown, provided by the Angelic Kings of DES, the Twenty-Sixth Aire, reaffirms the qualities of the purple cloak and also my path ahead.

By Epping Forest, North East London
Sunday, 28 April 1996, 4:00 p.m.

The Twenty-fourth Æthyr NIA
Angelic Kings • ZARNAAH • LAVAVOT • ZINGGEN

FIRST VISION

I am in a hilly region with green grass and granite outcrops. There is a cool breeze.

A small flaxen-haired child appears and I request to be taken around the Aire. The imagery becomes absolutely overwhelming, illusion after illusion. I see dark blue double doors and I feel utterly soporific, even while standing. I perform the

---

[67]. Hod (Glory) and Netzach (Victory), so at this point, I am truly on their threshold. For the sephira Hod occupies the 24th, 23rd and 22nd Æthyrs and Netzach the 21st, 20th and 19th. These facts were unknown before the scrying began.

Qabalistic Cross in an attempt to normalise things. This did not work, so I return to the Temple of the Aires and re-enter the Aire.

A vast corridor stretches ahead. A door opens to reveal an endless riot of images. Everything is very public. There are crowds of people engaged in numerous activities. There are many buildings and markets teaming with life. I begin to drift and the situation begins to ease. I am now flying away from the jumble. The Sun is high in the sky. Glorious lands of gold are below me – all is gold.

It is idyllic. I feel as if I am gathering power for TOR, the Twenty-Third Æthyr. Beauty and warmth enrich me. I feel a perpetual smile and that I am leaving the old life with its material temptations. Now and then I have a vision of myself. Is this the Golem, or a reflection of myself that must be absorbed in order to progress? One must recognise past habits and experiences no longer of use. Atonement for misdeeds can be attained by acknowledging them and taking them to one's breast.

I now have a sword. I am sitting with this, dressed in the purple cloak with the gold crown from VTI on my head.

During the closing ceremonies for this session, I distribute power from the Aire at the end of the Lesser Banishing Ritual of the Pentagram in the hope that everyone can help improve themselves and leave behind all the debris in their lives.

By Epping Forest, North East London
Saturday, 25 May 1996, 3:30 p.m.

SECOND VISION

I enter the Æthyr. The air is cool and the atmosphere is ethereal. I am in the same place as before with the green hills and the granite outcrops. I bow to the Angelic Kings and I sense a glory above.

I obtain an all-round around vision of myself as I travel through the Aire. Circulating the Aire enables one to see all its aspects. At the same time, I am encircling myself, thereby obtaining a vision of my whole self, rather than just looking ahead somewhat blinkered. The Aire is oneself – circular, with neither a definite beginning nor end. It is a complete being, coexisting with oneself. Once the circle is complete one can progress with the journey.

I ascend in a column of smoke or mist. The Angelic Kings are seated at a table ahead of me. I am cleansed by golden light in which I blossom.

I have my gift of the sword, the "Reward of the Aire", from my previous visit to NIA, for which I am very grateful. I am ready for the next stage of the journey.

By Epping Forest, North East London
Saturday, 1 June 1996, 10:30 a.m.

The Twenty-third Æthyr TOR ᘐᒐᘗ
Angelic Kings • ZARNAAH • LAVAVOT • ZINGGEN

On passing through the door, I put on the purple robe and gazed into the blue crystal in the casket on the pedestal, but see nothing of import. The initial mist still surrounds me. Suddenly, there is a massive thunderclap and the sword parts the mist, which then clears. There is a cataclysm in the sky like exploding suns. The sky is brilliant white.

These realms are unlike the Aires closer to the elemental domains. I am further within the Universe now. Everything is bathed in gold, glimmering and twinkling like drops of rain or dew reflecting the Sun.

The daily routine of progression from one event or task to the next has no place here. Time is different. Time, as on earth, does not apply.

I become aware of the Divine Breath. There is a spinning; it is a spin that gathers and disperses. It is the processing of existence: the breathing of the Divine. It is forever and everlasting.

There is an awakening within me of this action. I drink in the splendour. This whole process is within all things, whether animate or inanimate.

GOLD IN THE LIVES OF ALL.

As I was about to return, a ring with a large amethyst is placed on the third finger of my right hand. I give grateful thanks.

By Epping Forest, North East London
Saturday, 13 July 1996, 11:30 a.m..

The Twenty-Second Æthyr LIN Ꝫᘃᖴ
Angelic Kings • ARFAOLG • OLPAGED • ARFAOLG

It is a bright spring day. Birds are singing but there is still a slight mist. I wear the purple cloak. A grey-cowled figure appears.

"I am thy guide, the Grey Guide of LIN. My name is unimportant. I have been commissioned by the Angelic Kings to aid your penetration of the mysteries of this Æthyr."

He parts the mist and I am above the golden roofs of many cities. They are the wealth of the Earth transformed for the enrichment of the Divine. The wisdom of the Earth is absorbed by the inward breath.

The cities spin under me until there is just gold light of magnificence. It streams up through me to the Divine. I am the channel for the inward breath of earthly wisdom.

A flower, wonderful to behold, blossoms above me. Its divine essence will return through mankind to enrich the Earth with the outward breath.

I taste nectar. I have expanded and grown during this process.

Back before the door to the Temple, I thank the Grey Guide of LIN and hold the Orb from the casket aloft in reverence to the Secret of the Breath.

By Epping Forest, North East London
Friday, 30 August 1996, 3:30 p.m.

The Twenty-first Æthyr ASP ΩƮϾ

Angelic Kings • ARFAOLG • CADAAMP • ZURCHOL

"Come! There is no need for the cloak," I am told upon entering the Aire. I feel that I have shed a layer from myself.

I am standing on a ledge high in the mountains. The world is below me. I am standing on the edge of the world between the physical and the spiritual. I grow in stature through space. The atmosphere is still misty. My mind is slowly becoming one with the mist and, as a result, I can now perceive the complete structure of the world and its dependent life forms. The world is part of you and you are the world.

One has become the living soul of the world (the Nephesh)[68], not just the astral form, as eventually one will have insight into the spiritual realms beyond, from beginning to end.

LET THERE BE LIGHT IN THE WORLD!
The mist, with which the mind had united, suddenly clears and there is just

---

68. See Chapter 6 for information on the divisions of the soul.

brilliant golden light. Golden rays shine forth. This is the beginning of that insight into the realms of existence.

I am the Channel for the Light, which I glimpse for the briefest of moments.

Now everything fades and darkens and I am again before the door to the Temple ready to return.

By Epping Forest, North East London.
Thursday, 26 September 1996, 10:30 p.m.

THIS COMPLETES THE JOURNEY
THROUGH THE FIRST TEN ÆTHYRS.

CHAPTER NINE

THE AIRES FROM THE TWENTIETH (CHR) TO THE ELEVENTH (ICH)

The Twentieth Æthyr   CHR ℰ♡⃝13
Angelic Kings • GEBABAL • HONONOL • ALPUDUS

The wind is whistling. The bare branches of trees can be seen through the mist. The ground is rocky beneath the feet; there is a mist-filled chasm on my left.

I turn round and a warm, deep orange light glows in the distance. I hear the happy sound of piping. Is this the music of Ruach?[69] This is the first step towards the formation of the Soul and its gradual revelation and purification. There is such a long way to go.

I feel full of youthful vigour. There is a low mist, characteristic of early morning. It is the dawn of a new day. The sap is rising.

I look up through a funnel above and then I rise up through this. A magnificent brilliance overwhelms me as I reach the top of the funnel. It is a sun of white brightness. I am in a dream-like state as I rise through the funnel, but there was no drift. I continue to grow until I have a vision of the vast starry universe with which I co-existed along with the wonderful white brilliance.

I feel there is purity here. It is a truly different locale from the previous ten Æthyrs.

"You must work within this realm now", instruct the Angelic Kings.

Immediately, I rapidly descended to the door to the Temple. The Angelic Kings are waiting for me. I put on the purple cloak, so that it can absorb the knowledge I have gained before I return.[70]

By Epping Forest, North East London
Friday, 27 September 1996, 4:05 p.m.

---

69. See Chapter 6 for information on the divisions of the soul.
70. Also known as the The Cloak of Knowledge.

The Nineteenth Æthyr POP ΠΛΩ
Angelic Kings ARFAOLG • CADAAMP • ZINGGEN

I enter the Aire, throw the purple cloak around me and greet the Angelic Kings. The pale blue crystal stone in the casket glows before me. Then I take off the cloak. A light is rising like the Sun before me. It is golden, white brilliance. There are white clouds beneath me with mountain peaks peeping through.

I stand in the form of a cross suspended above the land of the Aire. For a moment I feel like The Hermit of the Tarot giving light to the world.

Now I am travelling through space and then, suddenly, I return to ground level and I am near the door of Aire. An eagle soars through the sky and a white, gold and silvery mist swirls around me. I am robed in white. I sense the interior of a vast gothic cathedral or is it a grove of tall trees arching above.

It would seem that I have encountered a power source. It must be harnessed for the good of the world, so that the work of the Divine can be undertaken throughout the planet. Notions of creativity and healing prevail. The power source must be contained. It must not be allowed to diffuse and disperse; otherwise all the energy will be lost.

I open the casket and the force enters the pale blue crystal that now glows a deep, bright, fiery red. It is ready for use. I must make sure that the force remains sealed within.

The Kings inform me that the following Æthyrs will provide instruction for the use and control of the power.

"You have done well", I am told.

And I become aware that the Gold Crown is upon my head and that I am wearing the purple cloak once again.

By Epping Forest, North East London
Saturday, 5 October 1996, 11:05 a.m.

The Eigteenth Æthyr ZEN ƷℸP
Angelic Kings • GEBABAL • ALPUDUS • ARFAOLG

Having passed through the door, I stand by the entrance wearing the crown and the purple cloak. The crystal is in the opened casket before me. All the knowledge from the Thirtieth to the Nineteenth Æthyrs is contained within.

I gaze into the mist that is always by the entrance. It clears.

I leave the cloak. I am totally naked. It is night time; the sky is clear. Whirling and spiralling winds engulf me. I am completely transparent, standing in the form of a cross above all.

Light dawns and I back into the Sun.[71] My head is the Sun. I feel benign and wish to care for all creatures. Rays from my outstretched arms flash and are like streaks of electricity. My body is a furnace of white light. It is possessed of an absolute purity.

I start to spin in order to distribute the power so that it is available for whomever is in need; wherever and whenever. This power is within all of us. It needs to be acknowledged and extracted. We must become responsible beings and aspire to this.

The spinning starts to slow. There is a cooling and then I am naked before the door to the Temple. I put on the purple cloak to enhance it with the knowledge gained from the journey. I close the casket. I feel energised and very excited. I wait until everything is calmer and then return.

By Epping Forest, North East London
Saturday, 26 October 1996, 11:35 a.m.

The Seventeenth Æthyr   TAN ᴣ✦ᴊ
Angelic Kings • ZIRACAH • OLPAGED • ZARZILG

I enter the Aire and the three Angelic Kings are before me. They greeted me as follows:

"We are waiting for you. Pray come. We will show you our realm."

There is a white ground mist. It is slightly windy and clouds are moving slowly overhead. The Sun is in the distance. Its rays are shining over the mist. I feel warm and have a sense gloriousness. I stand in the form of a cross.

The Angelic Kings are standing in front of me. They open the sky with their arms performing semi-circular arcs. They dissolve into the rays of the Sun.

The Sun comes closer. It is surrounded by a beautiful, pale yellow light, which begins to encircle me.

---

71. Tiphareth occupies the 18th, 17th and 16th Æthyrs. This fact was not known before the meditations began. The Sun is the planet of this sephira and its imagery is a major feature of the travels in these three Aires

I feel that I am in a place beyond Time itself. Everything is rarefied, pure, and exquisite. I am transparent, but somehow my form generates a pale yellow light.

Suddenly, I am walking on earth in a green field. Everything around me contains glints of gold - the leaves of the trees, blades of grass, even the rabbits, which are watching me.

This light is in all things. It is normally hidden and is only revealed when the purity of basic existence is realised. The Fall obscured this light and hid it from mankind, plunging everything into darkness. To become aware of this light in the depth of the darkness is the first stage on the journey to spiritual enlightenment.

The yellow light sees all. Once it sees the light or flame burning within all things, it can reveal the flame to all and once this awareness is gained, the knowledge can be passed to others. It is the spreading of the fire of spirituality.

By Epping Forest, North East London
Sunday, 3 November 1996, 4:30 p.m.

The Sixteenth Æthyr   LEA

Angelic Kings • ZIRACAH • HONONOL • ARFAOLG

FIRST VISION

The Sun is bright. Dressed in the purple cloak, I look into the pale blue crystal. I become aware of the special clasp with mysterious symbol on the cloak, I descend into the crystal. There are many dancing colours. It is like the whirling of a brightly painted carousel. I am naked under the cloak and feel sexual power, arousal, and the vibrancy of the life force. It is this intensity that leads to the generation of the physical form. It is the source of creation for the physical body.

A vortex of flame stretches above me into the Aires beyond. The cloak holds the physical body together. It physicalises the body. One is a physical creature. Once the cloak is removed, the physical form is no longer constrained. It dissipates and becomes a pure force, a spiritual creature.

The positive forces of creation as defined by the physical body on earth (namely: sexual arousal, erection, inner tensions). I am receiving and giving the creative force as an asexual being / man-woman / the hermaphrodite / the conjoining of natures / combination.

The Sixteenth Aire to the Thirtieth Aire deals with the creation of the physical being. This has just been "undone" on these travels. The journey from the Fifteenth to the First Aire is the creation of the spiritual or, rather, the refinement and purification leading to union with Divine forces.

Note

It is important not to give in to the physical gratification of sexual desire during this meditation, as this will immediately cast the scryer back into the physical world of their own particular sexuality. In this Aire, the key is asexuality and spiritual progression. Indulge one's desires in whatever way satisfies after the ceremony and only after the record has been written, if the need still exists.

By Epping Forest, North East London
Friday, 11 November 1996, 11:30 p.m.

SECOND VISION

With the first working in LEA, I arrived at the midway point on the journey through the Æthyrs. I am now at the crossover into the upper world of the individuality. The personality is of the lower worlds. This point is the meeting with the Holy Guardian Angel or the upper self. The second vision of LEA endeavours to take the first tentative steps into the higher realms. It enables me to revise my opinion towards my former workers, who were banished after working DES, the Twenty-Sixth Aire and who have now turned their backs on the study of Angelic Magic. Renewed contact is welcome, when they are ready.

I am on the top of a mountain at sunset. I am wearing the purple cloak of the Æthyrs and the crystal is before me. Clouds billow in the sky and there is much warm air from the setting Sun.

I look to the higher realms. I see cathedrals, the spires of places of worship, temples, pagodas and stupas; dazzling white marble buildings stretching into the distance. I am above this vista and I am neither able to see the ground nor, consequently, the diurnal round of the inhabitants. This vision of the holy buildings represents their sacred desires, their collective worship, their prayers and devotions for aspiring to unite (or reunite) with the spirit of creation.

Layers peel away. I witness brighter and brighter suns, each one more glorious. Alternatively, it is the same sun becoming purer and more brilliant, the brilliance manifesting more intensely with each stage of the purification.

Troubles are burned away; the rubbish is swept away by the shining pure force of the spirit which is the source of existence. The journey to the supreme state is the sacrifice. This is the initiatory point. Once there is acknowledgement of the past and acceptance of the errors committed, progress is possible.

I throw off the cloak and stand in the form of a cross. I am bathed in a brilliant light. I perform the Qabalistic Cross - ATEH [Ah teh]; MALKUTH [Mahl-kooth]; VE-GEBURAH [Vay-geb-or-rah]; VE GEDULAH [Vay-ged-you-lah] – the Cross of the Elements on Earth. This connects directly to the spiritual roots of the elements or the Four Holy Living Creatures in Kether: the Lion (Leo / Fire); the Eagle (Scorpio / Water); Man (Aquarius / Air); the Bull (Taurus / Earth). I omit the closing line of the ritual and at this point now perform the Qabalistic Cross again to bring down the force direct from Kether – ATEH; MALKUTH; saying VE GEDULAH instead, as I touch the right shoulder and then VE-GEBURAH, as I touch the left. I am standing as Adam Kadmon, the archetypal or primordial man, so that the right-hand pillar of the Tree of Life diagram is now the right-hand side of my body. I have walked into the tree as opposed to observing it from an earthly perspective.

I sense a rising and light becoming brighter. Suddenly, all is compressed to a pin point and I awake as the Eye of the Universe. The closed eye of *the Ain Soph*, Infinity or the Endless One has become aware of its own existence and progression from the negative existence or the "No-Thing" of the *Ain*.

This realisation is known as the *Ain Soph Aur* or Limitless Light.

I descend gathering layers of existence. I stand at the door of the temple sensing my body is full of flecks of gold within. I clasp my hands together and complete the ritual saying LE-OLAM, AMEN [Lay-orh-lahm, Ar-men].

By Epping Forest, North East London
Sunday, 9 January 1997, 3:30 p.m.

The Fiftheenth Æthyr   OXO   ⌐Γ⌐
Angelic Kings • ZARZILG • LAVAVOT • ARFAOLG

As soon as I enter the Aire, I find that I am automatically wearing the cloak. It infuses me with the knowledge gained so far, thereby enabling me to continue the journey without a break or regression.

There is a high wind. Gold-flecked clouds swirl overhead and there is a golden light beyond. I find myself rising, seemingly shedding layers of being the higher I go until I become a transparent star-being in space. I co-exist in divine space, but obviously not as one with the Divine.

Now I am in a crystal temple. The hard floor is transparent and stars are all around the crystal structure. The crystal walls exist because I am still in physical existence. However, they will disintegrate eventually. I will be able to witness this, even though I am, at present, a seemingly transparent being that cannot shatter while still having a corporeal existence on another plane. When the walls do break, co-existence with the Divine will commence.

The crystal temple allows me to be aware of the physical body and I can see the limitations. I am the crystal temple of OXO. It is the half-way point in the journey from TEX to LIL. The journey to the upper realms now begins. The physical world must be abandoned.

I am matter in space. I am unfolding. "The Spark Within" has become larger and brighter, absorbing the old physical shell. As the journey progresses, the spark becomes dominant. One is now the spark, whereas hitherto the physical body was dominant and the spark was hidden within. The realisation of its existence is the beginning of spiritual development, however apparently insignificant that realisation may seem.

The Æthyr OXO is the Aire of Transformation.

By Epping Forest, North East London
Saturday, 15 February 1997, 11:00 a.m.

The Fourteenth Æthyr VTA
Angelic Kings • GEBABAL • ALPUDUS • ARFAOLG

The Fourteenth Æthyr is an ethereal realm – an inspirational Aire. It is within one's power to accomplish all things. The Aire enables progress and points the way to the Divine, dispensing aid and assistance as required. I am relaxing in an emotional world, attempting to understand and control the emotions. I draw energy to transform the feelings into a positive outpouring.

Nothing is achieved by negative ideas and thoughts, which are self-consuming.
DO WHAT THOU WILT.

The Microcosm carries out the will of the Macrocosm, yet the two are synonymous. Each exists as the other. *Thou* is synonymous with the Self, completely in tune with the Divine Will. [72]

All guilty feelings must be rejected, as they are too damaging and draining. Just accept the actions which created the guilt and move on. Do not dwell on the matter. The nature of the guilt and the length of time it is endured will vary according to the gravity of the error. This will also govern one's ability to acknowledge, accept and finally absorb the guilt.

The three Angelic Kings appear as one being. I join them and embrace them in mutuality and experience a shared transparency.

The Communion of VTA.
Our combined being holds a chalice aloft. I separate myself from the Kings and gold rains down on me. I stand in the rain until I become a glowing, golden entity instilled with the virtues of VTA. I give thanks and return.

By Epping Forest, North East London.
Saturday, 8 March 1997, 11:10 a.m.

The Thirteenth Æthr ZIM ᛐ 7 P
Angelic Kings • LAVAVOT • OLPAGED • ALPUDUS

I walk the earth as transparent star-being with the fire of the spirit within. I feel timeless, roving space and the time zones. I am anywhere and everywhere simultaneously. I am at once, one star and all of the stars. It is like being the mind of the universe, except that the universal mind is far more expansive than the star-being.

By becoming denser, I can descend through the Æthyrs to the world of the elements. I am in a position in which I am able to undertake deeds in the lower Aires for the benefit of the planet.

Warning
Beware of becoming power-obsessed. This would work against any ostensibly good work by effectively rendering it worse than useless.

By Epping Forest, North East London
Saturday, 12 April 1997, 10:45 a.m.

---

72. See also, DEO – the Seventh Æthyr, below.

The Twelfth Æthyr   LOE
Angelic Kings • ZURCHOL • CADAAMP • ZIRACAH

Storm clouds swirl around me. I grow to a tremendous height. The Angelic Kings show me the world.

"*Ultimately, thou must relinquish thy worldly existence, I am told. Everything must go from the very depths to the sublime: the beautiful, the ugly, Mother Nature herself, palaces, hovels, from every precious jewel to the last glittering bauble.*"

Nothing takes precedence, when leaving the world of matter, except the pure, which can help prepare the mind for The Departure.

The Process of Departing

The world is a miniscule dot in the heavens. It is like a small model at my feet and reveals the Sun and blazing fires in the East; seas in the South; lush green vegetation in the West; and mountains to the North. The quarters must be abandoned one at a time at the correct hour which will only become apparent during the leaving process. Obviously, an intimation of the experience of the journey to the supreme spiritual state is not possible. It is a transmutation and an everlasting elixir. It is a perpetual regeneration of the self, forever enriched by the experience of the material world. It is beauty absolute.

My form diminishes in readiness for The Departure. However, on this occasion I return to the Enochian temple of the Aires.

By Epping Forest, North East London
Saturday, 10 May 1997, 11:30 a.m.

The Eleventh Æthyr   ICH
Angelic Kings • LAVAVOT • ZURCHOL • HONONOL

As soon as I enter the Aire, the mist clears. I stand in the form of the cross, looking at a brilliant rising Sun.

I am facing East and I am drawn towards the midst of the Sun. I feel utterly purified by the rays.

I turn to the South. I am deep within a mountainous landscape. I plunge downwards into the darkness of the lower slopes. Then I slowly rise again and I am once again in the brightness feeling refreshed and renewed. I stand in a new landscape with fresh green grass under my feet.

I turn to the West. Now I am standing in a fast moving stream being washed over and over again. The water stops running, the Sun shines. I am completely covered with water droplets within which are glistening golden jewels of light.

I turn to the North. I stand in a vortex. Wind is drying me and the impurities are being whirled away in order to make way for brand new growth. The leafless branches of trees become lushly green again. The old, withered vegetation has gone. Young, delicate leaves shoot forth in the spring. Fresh life is in the offing. The circuit of the Æthyr is complete. The Angelic Kings lay their hands on me transferring qualities of strength, fortitude, courage, love, devotion and enlightenment.

The Sun is slowly setting on the world I know.

I bow to the Kings.

By Epping Forest, North East London
Wednesday, 17 September 1997, 11:55 p.m.

I HAVE COMPLETED TWO-THIRDS OF MY JOURNEY THROUGH THE ÆTHYRS.

CHAPTER TEN

THE AIRES FROM THE TENTH (ZAX) TO THE FIRST (LIL)

The Tenth Æthy ZAX
Angelic Kings • ZINGGEN • ALPUDUS • ZARZILG

The mist clears rapidly when I enter the Aire. In front of me three blasted oak trees stand silhouetted against the sky. A strange being suddenly danced by from left to right, but it was so fast that it was impossible to discern any details of its form.

I am myself, nothing more, nothing less. It is essential to be as such at all times. I find myself in an old oak panelled room. There is a bright halo around me and I realise that I am in the Temple of the Tenth Aire. The panelled walls fade and I am standing on a circular dais of polished black onyx. Pillars of onyx surround me. A Brilliance in the distance slowly approaches. The Temple is a bridge across worlds. I wave to my mother as I pass across the worlds. There is an inner sadness as I fly through space.

My whole vision is of a sky full of massive stars that are seemingly fused together and yet, at the same time, are separate entities. I have a fleeting vision of an immense golem. It is the objective totality of oneself containing all past faults and failures as well as the victories. Suddenly, the dusty shell of its body crumbles and falls to the floor. Everything is covered in grey dust. Now, I am a body of light. I walk by the husk that was the golem. The body with all its rules and regulations is no longer needed.

It is a new beginning. I step free from the old order, revitalised. The stars of the Universe are within me. The way forward is to move away from the past and its arbitrary existence and fuse with the Divine in glory.

All souls will combine becoming the "Great Inward Breath" and then breathe out to the World of Matter and all its component parts which, in their individual existences, do not realise that they are actually united as part of the universal whole. These very actions ensure that origins are clouded and forgotten.

However, on experiencing this, I believe that I can return to the World of Matter. I know my origins and that I have the Divine spark within as I fuse once more with matter. Nevertheless, although the glow is present, there is still a long way to go before I have complete understanding and realisation.

Now I am back at the door to the Enochian Temple waiting to return. The three blasted oaks have a point of brilliance within.*

By Epping Forest, North East London
Sunday, 2 May 1998, 10:55 a.m.

* Later that day, I walked by a blasted oak silhouetted against a moonlit sky. My vision was thereby earthed and I knew that I had truly returned to the physical world.

The Ninth Æthyr   ZIP   ΟZΡ
Angelic Kings • HONONOL • LAVAVOT • ZARZILG

Tall cliffs loom ahead. The sky is bright. I climb to the top of the cliffs and can see all the lands of the world below me. The sky clouds over and a mist billows around my feet. I am a pure, golden being. A sense of gentleness pervades all. There is nothing either harsh or grating. Golden balls bounce over the clouds now hiding my vision of the world below.

I am being transported to ethereal worlds, being guided by the stars. I am in a space beyond the physical. There is a sense of boundaries being passed and lots of junk from the past is shed as each boundary is crossed. I drift as I travel to a higher plane. This is the essence of this Æthyr on the other side of The Abyss.

I have visions of slaughtering. It is a cleansing and the burying of ghosts from the past. Now a blazing fire thoroughly purifies everything, creating a *tabula rasa* or a clean slate. Nothing is left of the old life; it is not required any more. It is much too embedded in the material world to allow any forward movement. One can only progress if all debts have been paid and the slate erased.

I am ready for the next stage of the journey.

> By Epping Forest, North East London
> Friday, 24 July 1998, 10:00 p.m.

The Eighth Æthyr   ZID ƆⅬP
Angelic King • GEBABAL • OLPAGED • ZARZILG

I am in a high place, standing in the form of a cross. The Sun is straight ahead. Still in the form of the cross, I take off and soar beyond the Earth and the stars. Then I am swooping down again. As before, earthly things seem to have no importance. There is nothing drawing me back. Life passes by, but one still remains. I look beyond to the glory of the heavens and to the Unmanifest, where one is no more. I feel as if I am an angelic being and guide. I am possessed of a silver-white translucency.

My work is to collect souls; to rescue people from a return to manifestation after their life on earth is over.

My purpose is to give hope. I am a fixture on earth. I slowly put on layers of existence, so that I can become indistinguishable from mortals. This allows me to aid them with the journey towards spirituality.

> By Epping Forest, North East London
> Monday, 5 July 1999, 3:15 p.m.

Note
In retrospect, these results could appear rather ambitious. However, may be not.

The Seventh Æthyr   DEO ⌐ⅬƆ
Angelic Kings • ZARNAAH • HONONOL • ZINGGEN

A quiet, peaceful and still evening. It is sunset. The Sun can be seen setting through trees, which are silhouetted against the red-gold light. I stand on the edge of a cliff-top, bathed in the light of the setting Sun. Yet again, I stand in the form of a cross and vibrate the name of the Aire and the three Angelic Kings. The sky parts.

It is no longer sunset; the sky is a brilliant blue with many white clouds.

Despite the over-ambitious feelings experienced in the Eighth Æthyr, there is still a part of me that longs for the Earth. I am, after all, a creature of the Earth. The spiritual flame burns in us all. The Flame grows, fed by the experience of manifestation that in turn illuminates the planet and nourishes the Godhead, which then further enriches the earth and its creatures as a consequence. If a person connects with this divine current of the Flame within, they will act in accordance with the Divine Will. This is the origin of Aleister Crowley's *Law of Thelema:*
Do what thou wilt, shall be the whole of the Law.

Driven by the True Will of the Divine, one becomes a benefit to all and able to live in keeping with the Flame which will burn all the spiritual impurities from the body. In this way the body can become the universe, limitless, and able to expand the Divine being within.

By Epping Forest, North East London
Friday, 13 August 1999, 11:30 p.m.

At this point, the exploration of the Æthyrs ceases until 2008.

The Sixth Æthyr   MAZ   P✗E
Angelic Kings • GEBABAL • ARFAOLG • GEBABAL

FIRST VISION

I am standing in dark hills on the edge of a white, silvery sea. Beyond, the Sun is setting. It is a huge fire ball and the sky is filled with a deep orange glow. The light is blinding and I am drawn towards the glowing orange of the Sun until my whole vision is totally filled with its light.

There is a pinpoint of white brilliance in the centre. Now I am drawn towards this. I am a golden-orange being. I have no physical limitations, but I do not become a brilliant white form at this stage (but see the Second Vision in this Aire).

I slowly draw back into the darkness. The Sun has set and I am before the door of the Temple of the Aires. Dark green ivy grows around the door, forming a bower. I return to the temple.

By Epping Forest, North East London
Wednesday, 17 September 2008, 14:30 p.m.

Yet again, the work ceases for almost 10 years.

SECOND VISION

The mist is quite dense and in front of me I can just about make out the shadowy forms of the three Angelic Kings. They step aside and take my hands - GEBABAL (who has a dual responsibility in this Aire) holds the left one and ARFAOLG the right.

It is still misty. The terrain is crunchy underfoot as we walk. Suddenly, GEBABAL and ARFAOLG leave me and I am surrounded by a bright , blinding brilliance containing golden rays of light. As they depart, the Angelic Kings inform me:

"You are now on your own. We can no longer be of assistance. Henceforward, you must make your own way unaided."

I am a pinprick of light in the white blaze. I am travelling fast within it. Swirling galaxies, solar systems and rotating planets are below me and the light is now a pinkish, pale purple colour. I realise that I am actually one of the planets. I am spinning and spinning, gradually turning into a firm body, slowly solidifying and crystallising.

"How can I return now?" I ask the Kings.

"Take this knowledge of formation (the Roar of Creation) back with you", they reply.

Steadily, I build up a covering of flesh and blood until I resume my earthly form. I am back from the Roar of Creation. The secret is within us all.

Now a peacefulness pervades all. I give thanks and pass through the doorway to the Temple of the Aires.

Thorpe Hamlet, Norwich
Tuesday, 1 May 2018, 14:45 p.m.

The Fifth Æthyr LIT ⟁⟀

Angelic Kings • OLPAGED • ALPUDUS • ZINGGEN

    The mist clears and the three Angelic Kings stand aside as I pass into the Fifth Aire.

    Again there is an incredible brightness everywhere. I become transfixed and immobile.

    "*Go!*" shout the Kings who together push me hard from behind. I drift and witness unidentifiable historical scenes flashing in front of me. Recovering, I find myself in a mist on a rocky, sparsely grassed mountainside.

    The mist clears and below me I see glittering golden cities stretching to the horizon. They must be for everyone, not just for a chosen few. Before long I realise these cities are just too dazzling to be of value to anyone. One is blinded by all the shimmering gold and seduced by the glamour of the riches and the stunningly wide vistas. For now there stands behind me a row of skeletons in darkness. They are the shells of physicality. They are the remnants of the material world. The dazzling cities will ultimately become like this.

    I go down to a glittering city. A massive golden temple is ahead on the horizon. I cannot reach the temple. Is it real? I realise that I must be content with what I have and that I must not yearn for golden temples in the distance. This is especially so, now there is a wholeness within.[73] Ignore this at one's peril or suffer detrimental consequences. Upon these thoughts I made my way back.

    Thorpe Hamlet, Norwich
    Wednesday, 9 May 2018, 11:45 p.m.

The Fourth Æthyr PAZ ℘⚹Ω

Angelic Kings • LAVAVOT • LAVAVOT • ARFAOLG

    FIRST VISION

    A clear light reveals a quiet and peaceful scene. There are no unusual features. Suddenly, the sky darkens and a massive thunderclap booms. Two streaks of lightning flash across the sky followed by a downpour, which soaks me to the skin. The Angelic Kings throw the purple Cloak of Knowledge over me and place the gold crown on my head. I had not worn these together since my travels in ZEN, the Eighteenth Æthyr.

---

73. The Knowledge of Creation. See the *Sixth Æthyr*- Second Vision above.

I walk though the rain. A figure appears. The person is asexual, as they are neither noticeably male nor female. They are clad in skin-tight silver clothing and stand behind a table like the Magician of the Tarot. They hold a wand in their right hand and a sword in the left. The figure starts waving them from side to side and over and around their head. The movements become faster and faster until they are no longer discernible.

Suddenly, there is a great explosion of blinding light followed immediately by an absolute calmness. Nothing (No-Thing) exists, except for pure light.

At this point, I have an overwhelming desire to return. LAVAVOT (who has a dual function in this Aire) said that I must contemplate for a while. Next I hear the beating of wings and I am immediately taken to the door of the Aire. I am welcomed by the other kings, who pronounce:

"You have witnessed deep mysteries. Return forthwith and ruminate."

They wave and I return somewhat puzzled

Thorpe Hamlet, Norwich
Tuesday, 15 May 2018, 2:00 p.m.

SECOND VISION

"*Welcome to the Lands of Creation*", says a royal-blue robed figure as I enter the Aire. I feel ageless. I survey the scene before me, but once again there is nothing of interest. Everything is fused with pure light. I sense neither a beginning nor an end. Nothing has been formed. My body is transparent, so I am also without form or as the blue-robed figure tells me, "*So you are not*".

As I have no physical body, I am part of the scene. I am one with it. I cannot move.

ARFAOLG throws a flashing red and orange cloak around me that creates a form enabling me to have a body to return with. The Angelic King holds up a diamond-shaped clay tablet bearing this sign.*

I remove the cloak. I am naked. My new form has an urge to create and this leads to an intense erotic desire. The kings surround me until the force is spent and the creative desire fulfilled. I will have to return soon.

Was this the creation of the Element of Fire itself? I am ablaze – a being of flame. I am radiant from the fire. Nearing the door of the Aire, I feel very warm and I am still smouldering as the fire dies down. I am like a glowing ember, as I pass back into the Temple

Normal room temperature slowly returns, but my hands still feel aflame until the final closing ceremony. Afterwards I remain warm for some time.
I have just visited the House of the Flame.

* The sign is the seal or sigil of the Fourth or Northern Quarter of the Great Table of Earth. During the angelic communications of Dee and Kelley, the appearance of such seals heralded the reception of each of the four tablets of the Great Table. The four seals are:

EAST

SOUTH

WEST

NORTH

16. The Four Seals of the Watchtowers

Kelley noted: "*In the last corner of this earthly Table appeareth a little round smoke, as big as a pins head*". [74]

The fourth and final quarter is sometimes represented by the final H of the IHVH, which can indicate manifestation and, in this case, that my physical body is recreating itself.

Thorpe Hamlet, Norwich
Wednesday, 16 May 2018, 12:30 a.m.

The Third Æthyr ZOM ᴇʟP
Angelic Kings • ZARZILG • ALPUDUS • LAVAVOT

Upon entering the Æthyr, I immediately experience the Four Elements.

FIRE – I am walking along a path with flames burning on both sides. I feel very warm.

WATER – I encounter a stream. Coolness and calmness pervades all. The blazing path is behind me now. The light fades and it becomes cold and dark. I return to the blaze. ZARZILG appears and gives me the purple cloak and the gold crown, which somehow looks smaller than usual.

AIR – I am now swept along by a strong wind. I have left the House of The Flame.

EARTH – I am deep in the earth. My cloak has become black in colour. I see the head of a goat, possibly a mask. All physical things originate in the deep earth, from which our bodies are made, layer upon layer.

I decided that I did not need another layer imposed. There are many old roots remaining in the earth from dead vegetation. I see a bed of Narcissus daffodils, all in flower.[75] I pick some and give one to each Angelic King. They smile and laugh. I want to leave, but cannot. The Angelic Kings have aided my rebirth and regeneration as a spiritual form of the Four Elements. The flower is my thanks for this to

Fire: ZARZILG
Water: ALPUDUS
Air: LAVAVOT
Earth: This is myself – THE REGENERATE.

---

74. *T&FR*, p.173.
75. The Narcissus is the flower of rebirth, renewal and new beginnings. It is one of the earliest bulbs to appear and as such symbolises the coming of Spring

I am a kind of spiritually reborn version of the elements. I take off from a cliff top and below me are the physical forms of the four elements. My cloak is now white.

I circle and land before the doorway to the Temple of the Aires. ZARZILG takes my cloak and I return feeling warm. However, once back in the temple the temperature drops and there is a coldness in the air.

Thorpe Hamlet, Norwich
Tuesday, 29 May 2018, 2:30 p.m.

The Second Æthyr   ARN ƷƐ⸗

Angelic Kings • ZARNAAH • ZIRACAH • ZIRACAH

FIRST VISION

Having passed through the doorway into the Aire, I am immediately informed by the Angelic Kings:

"Do not forget that you are now the spiritual form of the four elements and as such you are the combined force of their power."

I stand in a silvery light in the form of a cross. I start to spin and become the crystal being. There was nothing else to do. I am the spirit of the elements and cannot be restrained by any means. I raise my arms and call out the names of the Angelic Kings.

A loud thunderclap followed by a heavy downpour of rain washes away my crystal form and I am one with the Aire. I am unable to progress, so I ask to return. Suddenly, I am a blazing ball of fire. I am thrown back to the door to the Temple.

Thorpe Hamlet, Norwich
Tuesday, 5 June 2018, 2.00p.m.

SECOND VISION

The Angelic Kings are dressed in grey-white cowled robes. They bid me to go ahead into the Aire and stand back to let me pass. Endless mundane images assail me until I am overcome with sadness. I call upon the Kings to stop the drift.

"Do not live in the past, otherwise you cannot progress", they respond.

"Forward!" they shout in unison.

I take off at great speed and I am soon high above the Earth. I become transparent, gathering layers of air around me as I travel. Then the vision is over and I am propelled back to the door of the Aire.

Thorpe Hamlet, Norwich
Tuesday, 12 June 2018, 1.00 p.m.

THIRD VISION

As I enter the Aire, Angelic Kings welcome me back. The mist clears and all is in sunlight, although I am not aware of the Sun. I am amidst tropical vegetation near a waterfall. I am a transparent being trailing a stream of minute golden specks of light over everything. But then I realise that the specks are not just on the surface, but are actually deep within. They are the inner sparks of divine creation within all things, both animate and inanimate. All is wondrous: everything is full of the golden sparks. However, the sparks fade with the increasing density of the material world until they can no longer be seen. When the awareness of their presence has gone, they are forgotten. Nevertheless, it is possible to reconnect with the sparks through the triumph of The Will. Now one has the ability to embrace the most hideous and disgusting thing, for even that has those divine sparks within itself, despite the outward appearance.

The vision extols the glories and magnificence of creation.

"Take it all back within you", the Angelic Kings tell me, *"Do not shed it like a snake skin."*

Even though the (divine) sparks dim as I approach the door of the Aire, the awareness of their presence must not be forgotten.

Thorpe Hamlet, Norwich,
Tuesday, 12 June 2018, 3.00p.m.

The First Æthyr   LIL   ⌀⏉⌀
Angelic Kings • ZARZILG • ZINGGEN • ALPUDUS

As I stand before the door to the Aires, it takes on a golden glow that quickly spreads in strands, interweaving with the silver walls of the temple. I pass through the door and the Angelic Kings stand before me. ZARZILG bows, saying, *"Come with me"*.

I am totally surrounded by a pulsating golden light filled with myriads of golden specks. I can see whirling solar systems and become aware that I am standing on the edge of a vortex looking down into it.

Then I am in a subterranean cave full of glittering jewels – a complete spectrum of colours. It is as if the all the colour scales of the Four Worlds of the Qabalistic Tree of Life are present in the form of scintillating gemstones. The dazzling scene causes me to drift and I call upon LIL and the Angelic Kings to stabilise myself.

I am transported through golden skies and I rest in the glory. Clouds with golden linings now surround me and I realise that there is no need to be confined in a temple space anymore. Before me, a golden lady sits on a throne. She has a crown of gold on her head and wears a golden, finely pleated cloak. Her name is ENIAH and she is the Angel or Goddess of the Watchtowers of the Four Quarters. Suddenly she throws open the golden cloak and I am confronted by a glittering, resplendent array of colours, which gradually turns into a brilliant, blinding white light approaching from afar.

I feel I am reaching the end of my journey in LIL. The super celestial awaits beyond. I am being drawn towards it. The Angelic Kings tell me that, when I am ready, I can go, but I will not return. The Time must be right to make such a decision, whereby one relinquishes the trappings of the material world.

The pulsating light slowly comes closer. The Angelic Kings surround me, enveloping me. I must return now or remain forever. I know inherently that the time is not yet and so the light fades to gold and slowly goes into the earth to spiritually nourish the terrestrial world and its creatures.

There is a sudden lightening flash, a storm approaches, and I am back in front of the silver door to the Temple of the Aires. I thank the Angelic Kings for the insight into the higher realms for which I am truly grateful.

Thorpe Hamlet, Norwich
Tuesday, 19 June 2018, 2:30 p.m.

MY JOURNEY THROUGH THE THIRTY ÆTHYRS IS COMPLETE.

CHAPTER ELEVEN

THE ELEMENTS OF THE WATCHTOWERS AND THE THIRTHIETH AIRE (TEX)
A GROUP WORKING

This working took place at the Autumnal Equinox on Sunday, 21 September 2008 at the Atlantis Bookshop, Bloomsbury, London. There were six participants. The schedule for the session follows below. All timings are approximate.

ENOCHIAN WORKSHOP PROGRAMME

11.00 – 13.00 • Part 1
1. Binding of the Qliphoth
2. Opening Invocation
3. Elements of the East: Open Temple
4. Pathworking / Meditation
5. Close Temple

Record experiences

SHORT BREAK

5. Elements of the South: Open Temple
6. Pathworking / Meditation
7. Close Temple
8. Close Temple & Part 1 working

Record experiences

LUNCH

14.00 -17.00 • Part 2
1. Binding of the Qliphoth
2. Opening Invocation
3. Elements of the West: Open Temple
4. Pathworking/Meditation
5. Close Temple
Record experiences

SHORT BREAK

5. Elements of the North: Open Temple
6. Pathworking/Meditation
7. Close Temple
Record experiences

SHORT BREAK

8. TEX – THE THIRTIETH AIRE: Open Temple of the Aires
9. Angelic Key or Call for the Thirtieth Aire
10. Pathworking/wMeditation
11. Close Temple of the Aires
12. Closing Invocation
13. General Closing of Working
Write-up final log of the Session, followed by "back to earth" refreshments.

SECTION 1 – THE RITUAL
ELEMENTS OF THE EAST
1. QABALISTIC CROSS
2. BINDING OF THE QLIPHOTH

When we enter herein with all humility, let God the Almighty One enter into this place, by the entrance of an eternal happiness, of a Divine prosperity, of a perfect joy, of an abundant charity, and of an eternal salutation.

Let all the demons fly from this place, especially those who are opposed unto this work, and let the angels of peace assist and protect this place, from which let discord and strife fly and depart.

Magnify and extend upon us, O Lord, thy most holy name, and bless our conversation and our assembly.[76] Sanctify, O Lord, our humble entry herein, thou the Blessed and Holy One of the Eternal Ages.
Amen.

3. OPENING INVOCATION
JEHOVAH TZABAOTH
We invoke most earnestly and call upon your divine power, wisdom and goodness and through these, your twelve Mystical Names
ORO IBAH AOZPI
MOR DIAL HCTGA
MPH ARSL GAIOL (GAI-OL)
OIP TEAA PDOCE
We conjure and pray that your angelic spirits may be called forth from any and all parts of the universe. Let them come most swiftly,
And depart peacefully upon request; and let them give reverence and obedience before thy twelve Mystical Names, fulfilling all that is asked of them according to their virtues and powers.
JEHOVAH TZABAOTH
We thank thee.
Amen

4. OPENING SIGN
We enter the
5. TEMPLE OF THE EASTERN QUARTER
Standing in a square RED ROOM facing EAST.
Red Walls, Floor and Ceiling.
Before us is the Door to the Elemental World of the 4th Lesser Angle.
On the Door are the triangular Elemental Signs, one beneath the other in the order as given in Dee's diaries.
AIR
WATER
EARTH
FIRE

---

76. The version for more than one participant is employed here.

6. INVOCATION TO THE GOD OF THE EAST
ORO IBAH AOZPI

O Mighty God of the East, we pray in thy three holy names to guide us through thy Lesser Fourth Angle, that we may open our consciousness and gain insight of the four elements of the east, so enabling us to deploy their virtues for the good of all.
Amen

Contemplate and move towards the Red Door to the World of the Elements of the East.
The door becomes transparent.
Pass through. There is a mist before you.

7. STAND ON THE OTHER SIDE AS THE ANGELS OF THE ELEMENTS ARE INVOKED IN TURN TO SHOW US THE ELEMENTS OF THE EAST.

INVOCATION
Through the holy names of this lesser angle
AOVRRZ (A-O-UR-REZ)
ALOAI (A-LO-AY)
We invoke thee, angels of the East, so that each one of thee may reveal to us thy elemental domain, the creatures living therein and their use.

- ACCA – EMINENT ANGEL – *pray reveal to us the glories of the Eastern Air.*

The mist clears.
Now observe Acca's world for a short while.
The vision fades. The mist returns.
We thank thee ACCA.

- NPAT (EN-PE-AT) – ILLUSTRIOUS ANGEL – *pray show us the Eastern Waters.*

The mist clears.
Now observe Npat's world for a short while.
The vision fades. The mist returns.
We thank thee NPAT.

- OTOI (O-TOY) – DISTINGUISHED ANGEL – *pray show us the varied qualities of the Earth of The East.*

The mist clears.

Now observe Otoi's world for a short while.
The vision fades. The mist returns.
We thank thee OTOI.
• PMOX (P-MOX) – SHINING ANGEL – *pray show us the secret properties of the Eastern Fire.*
The mist clears.
Now observe Pmox's world for a short while.
The vision fades. The mist returns.
We thank thee PMOX.

Standing in front of the transparent Door,
We now thank the Angels before departing
AOVRRZ (A-O-UR-REZ)
ALOAI (A-LO-AY)
Gods of the Fourth Angle of the East, we thank thee and thy Angels of the Elements for thy aid:
ACCA
NPAT
OTOI
PMOX

Pray depart in peace to thy abodes.
May there ever be peace between us.
Amen

We now leave the World of the Elements of the East
Pass backwards through the Door into the Red Temple of the East.
The door becomes solid and the elemental signs fade there from.

8. CLOSE
ORO IBAH AOZPI
O Mighty God of the East, we thank thee for thy wisdom and guidance. Any understanding and knowledge gained of the elements of thy realm will be used beneficially for all.
The temple walls fade.

ORO IBAH AOZPI
In thy name I declare the Temple of the Eastern Quarter closed.

9. CLOSING OF THE VEIL
If any spirits be entrapped by this ceremony, pray depart in peace to thy abodes. May there ever be peace between us. We thank Thee.

10. QABALISTIC CROSS
Record experiences.

Short Break

ELEMENTS OF THE SOUTH

1. QABALISTIC CROSS
2. OPENING SIGN

We enter the

3. TEMPLE OF THE SOUTHERN QUARTER
Standing in a square WHITE ROOM facing SOUTH.
White Walls, Floor and Ceiling
Before us is the Door to the Elemental World of the 4th Lesser Angle.
On the Door are the triangular Elemental Signs, one beneath the other.
AIR
WATER
EARTH
FIRE

4. INVOCATION TO THE GOD OF THE SOUTH
MOR DIAL HCTGA

O Mighty God of the South, we pray in thy three holy names to guide us through thy lesser fourth angle, that we may open our consciousness and gain insight of the four elements of the south, so enabling us to deploy their virtues for the good of all. Amen

Contemplate and move towards the White Door to the World of the Elements of the South.
The door becomes transparent.
Pass through.
There is a mist before you.

5. STAND ON THE OTHER SIDE AS THE ANGELS OF THE ELEMENTS ARE INVOKED IN TURN TO SHOW US THE ELEMENTS OF THE SOUTH.

INVOCATION
Through the holy names of this lesser angle
SPMNIR (ESPE – EMNIR)
ILPIZ
We invoke thee, angels of the south, so that each one of thee may reveal to us thy elemental domain, the creatures living therein and their use.
- MSAL (EM - SAL) – EMINENT ANGEL – *pray reveal to us the glories of the Southern Air.*

The mist clears.

Now observe MSAL's world for a short while.

The vision fades. The mist returns.

We thank thee MSAL.
- IABA (YABA) – ILLUSTRIOUS ANGEL - *pray show us the Southern Waters.*

The mist clears.

Now observe IABA's world for a short while.

The vision fades. The mist returns.

We thank thee IABA.
- IZXP (IZ -EX – PE) – DISTINGUISHED ANGEL – *pray show us the varied qualities of the Earth of the South.*

The mist clears.

Now observe IZXP's world for a short while.

The vision fades. The mist returns.

We thank thee IZXP.
- STIM (ES – TEEM) – SHINING ANGEL – *pray show us the secret properties of the Southern Fire.*

The mist clears. Now observe STIM's world for a short while.

The vision fades. The mist returns.

We thank thee STIM.

Standing in front of the transparent Door.

We now thank the Angels before departing.

SPMNIR (ESPE – EMNIR)

ILPIZ
Gods of the Fourth Angle of the South, we thank thee and thy Angels of the Elements for thy aid:
MSAL (EM - SAL)
IABA (YABA)
IZXP (IZ - EX – PE)
STIM (ES – TEEM)
Pray depart in peace to thy abodes.
May there ever be peace between us.
Amen

We now leave the World of the Elements of the South.
Pass backwards through the Door into the White Temple of the South.
The door becomes solid and the elemental signs fade there from.

6. CLOSE
MOR DIAL HCTGA
O Mighty God of the South, we thank thee for thy wisdom and guidance. Any understanding and knowledge gained of the elements of thy realm will be used beneficially for all.
The temple walls fade.
MOR DIAL HCTGA
In thy name we declare the Temple of the Southern Quarter closed.

7. CLOSING OF THE VEIL
The ALPHA and the OMEGA, the beginning and the end, in the spirit of AZOTH We thank thee, O Mighty Ones, for thy aid. All wisdom gained will be used unselfishly and for the good.
If any spirits be entrapped in this place, pray depart in peace to thy abodes.
May there ever be peace between us.
We thank thee.
Amen [77]

8. QABALISTIC CROSS
Record experiences.

Lunch

---

77. A stronger closing is used here as the group vacated the temple for a break.

ELEMENTS OF THE WEST

1. QABALISTIC CROSS
2. BINDING OF THE QLIPHOTH

See Elements of the East for details.

3. OPENING INVOCATION

As the Temple was closed down for the break. It must be reopened again as before.

JEHOVAH TZABAOTH

We invoke most earnestly and call upon your divine power, wisdom and goodness. And through these your 12 mystical names

ORO IBAH AOZPI
MOR DIAL HCTGA
MPH ARSL GAIOL
OIP TEAA PDOCE

We conjure and pray that your angelic spirits may be called forth from any and all parts of the universe.
Let them come most swiftly
And depart peacefully upon request;
and let them give reverence and obedience before thy 12 mystical names, fulfilling all that is asked of them according to their virtues and powers.

JEHOVAH TZABAOTH
We thank thee.
Amen

4. OPENING SIGN

We enter the

5. TEMPLE OF THE WESTERN QUARTER

Standing in a square GREEN ROOM facing WEST.
Green Walls, Floor and Ceiling.
Before us is the Door to the Elemental World of the 4th Lesser Angle
On the Door are the triangular Elemental Signs, one beneath the other.
AIR
WATER

EARTH
FIRE

6. INVOCATION TO THE GOD OF THE WEST
MPH ARSL GAIOL (GAI – OL)
O mighty God of the West, we pray in thy three holy names to guide us through thy lesser fourth angle, that we may open our consciousness and gain insight of the four elements of the West, so enabling us to deploy their virtues for the good of all. Amen
Contemplate and move towards the Green Door to the World of the Elements of the West.
The door becomes transparent.
Pass through. There is a mist before you.

7. STAND ON THE OTHER SIDE AS THE ANGELS OF THE ELEMENTS ARE INVOKED IN TURN TO SHOW US THE ELEMENTS OF THE WEST.

INVOCATION
Through the holy names of this lesser angle
IAAASD (YA –A – ASDI)
ATAPA
We invoke thee, Angels of the West, so that each one of thee may reveal to us thy elemental domain, the creatures living therein and their use.
• XPEN (EX - PEN) – EMINENT ANGEL – *pray reveal to us the glories of the Western Air.*
The mist clears. Now observe XPEN's world for a short while.
The vision fades. The mist returns.
We thank thee XPEN.
• VASA – ILLUSTRIOUS ANGEL – *pray show us the Western Waters.*
The mist clears.
Now observe VASA's world for a short while.
The vision fades. The mist returns.
We thank thee VASA.
• DAPI – DISTINGUISHED ANGEL – *pray show us the varied qualities of the*

Earth of the West.
The mist clears.
Now observe DAPI's world for a short while.
The vision fades. The mist returns.
We thank thee DAPI.
- RNIL (UR - NEEL) – SHINING ANGEL- *pray show us the secret properties of the Western Fire.*
The mist clears.
Now observe RNIL's world for a short while.
The vision fades. The mist returns.
We thank thee RNIL.

Standing in front of the transparent Door
We now thank the Angels before departing
IAAASD (YA –A – ASDI)
ATAPA
Gods of the Fourth Angle of the West, we thank thee and thy Angels of the Elements for thy aid.
XPEN (EX - PEN)
VASA
DAPI
RNIL (UR - NEEL)
Pray depart in peace to thy abodes.
May there ever be peace between us.
Amen

We now leave the World of the Elements of the West.
Pass backwards through the Door into the GREEN TEMPLE OF THE WEST.

The door becomes solid and the elemental signs fade there from.

8. CLOSE
MPH ARSL GAIOL
O Mighty God of the West, we thank thee for thy wisdom and guidance. Any understanding and knowledge gained of the elements of thy realm will be used

beneficially for all.
The temple walls fade

MPH ARSL GAIOL
In thy name I declare the temple of the Western Quarter closed.

9. CLOSING OF THE VEIL
If any spirits be entrapped by this ceremony, pray depart in peace to thy abodes. May there ever be peace between us.

10. QABALISTIC CROSS
Record experiences

Short Break.

ELEMENTS OF THE NORTH

1. QABALISTIC CROSS

2. OPENING SIGN
We enter the

3. TEMPLE OF THE NORTHERN QUARTER
Standing in a square BILBERRY BLACK ROOM facing NORTH
Bilberry Black Walls, Floor and Ceiling.
Before us is the Door to the Elemental World of the 4th Lesser Angle.
On the Door are the triangular Elemental Signs, one beneath the other.
AIR
WATER
EARTH
FIRE

4. INVOCATION TO THE GOD OF THE NORTH
OIP TEAA PDOCE
O mighty God Of The North, we pray in thy three holy names to guide us through thy lesser fourth angle, that we may open our consciousness and gain insight of the four Elements of the North, so enabling us to deploy their virtues for the good of all.
Amen

Contemplate and move towards the Bilberry Black Door to the World of the

Elements of the North.
The door becomes transparent.
Pass through. There is a mist before you.

5. STAND ON THE OTHER SIDE AS THE ANGELS OF THE ELEMENTS ARE INVOKED IN TURN TO SHOW US THE ELEMENTS OF THE NORTH

INVOCATION
Through the holy names of this lesser angle
RZIONR (URZI – ONUR)
NRZFM (NUR – ZEFM)
We invoke thee, Angels of the North, so that each one of thee may reveal to us thy elemental domain, the creatures living therein and their use.

- ADRE – EMINENT ANGEL – *pray reveal to us the glories of the Northern Air.*

The mist clears.
Now observe ADRE's world for a short while.
The vision fades. The mist returns.
We thank thee ADRE.

- SISP (SIS – PE) – ILLUSTRIOUS ANGEL – *pray show us the Northern Waters.*

The mist clears.
Now observe SISP's world for a short while.
The vision fades. The mist returns.
We thank thee SISP.

- PALI – DISTINGUISHED ANGEL – *pray show us the varied qualities of the Earth of the North.*

The mist clears.
Now observe PALI's world for a short while.
The vision fades. The mist returns.
We thank thee PALI.

- ACAR – SHINING ANGEL- *pray show us the secret properties of the Northern Fire.*

The mist clears.
Now observe ACAR's world for a short while.
The vision fades. The mist returns.

We thank thee ACAR.
Standing in front of the transparent Door,
We now thank the Angels before departing.

RZIONR (URZI – ONUR)
NRZFM   (NUR – ZEFM)
Gods of the Fourth Angle of the North, we thank thee and thy Angels of the Elements for thy aid:
ADRE
SISP (SIS – PE)
PALI
ACAR
Pray depart in peace to thy abodes.
May there ever be peace between us.
Amen

We now leave the World of the Elements of the North.
Pass backwards through the door into the Bilberry Black Temple of the North.
the door becomes solid and the elemental signs fade away.

6. CLOSE
OIP TEAA PDOCE
O mighty God of the North, we thank thee for thy wisdom and guidance. Any understanding and knowledge gained of the elements of thy realm will be used beneficially for all.
The temple walls fade.
OIP TEAA PDOCE
In thy name I declare the temple of the Northern Quarter closed.

7. CLOSING OF THE VEIL
If any spirits be entrapped by this ceremony, pray depart in peace to thy abodes. May there ever be peace between us.

8. QABALISTIC CROSS
Record experiences.

Short Break.

TEX THE THIRTIETH AIRE
1. QABALISTIC CROSS
2. OPENING SIGN

We enter the

3. TEMPLE OF THE AIRES
- Facing East.
- Standing in Centre of a Shimmering White Silvery Circular Room.
- The Æthyrs are beyond.
- Before us is a SILVER DOOR – the Gateway to the Aires.
- This is the door to TEX the Thirtieth Æthyr.
- TEX IS ENGRAVED UPON THE DOOR (In both English and Angelic/Enochian characters if so desired).

Contemplate the Door.

4. CALL OF TEX THE THIRTIETH AIRE
1. English (or mother tongue, if easier)
2. Enochian

5. PATHWORKING

The doorway becomes transparent.
Move towards the door and cross the threshold into the Aire/Æthyr.
Stand in the silvery mist.
Names of the ANGELIC KINGS OF TEX are called:

ARFAOLG (AR- FA – OLDG)
ZARNAAH (ZAR – NA – AH)
HONONOL (HONO - NOL)
ZURCHOL (ZU- RE – KOL)

O Angelic Kings of Tex pray guide us through thy realm and grant an insight into its mysteries.
The mist clears.
Commence the journey into the Aire noting all impressions, visions and sounds.
DO NOT FORGET THE NAME OF THE AIRE AND THE ANGELIC KINGS.

Call upon them to halt drifting and to keep on the path.

6. CLOSE

When feel your journey is complete (or when directed) return to the transparent door the way you came.

The mist returns.

Stand looking into the Aire / Æthyr.

The names of the 4 Kings are called:

ARFAOLG (AR- FA – OLDG)
ZARNAAH (ZAR – NA – AH)
HONONOL (HO-NO – NOL)
ZURCHOL (ZU- RE – KOL)

We thank thee Angelic Kings of Tex, the Thirtieth Aire, for the safe transport through thy realm and the knowledge gained thereof. This we shall use beneficially for the earthly domain.

Pray depart in peace to thy abodes.

May there ever be peace between us.

Amen

Pass backwards through the doorway into the silvery Temple of the Aires.

THE DOOR CLOSES.

TEX fades there from.

Now the whole Temple fades.

The Temple of the Aires is closed

7. CLOSING OF THE VEIL
8. CLOSING INVOCATION

JEHOVAH TZABAOTH

In thy name and through these your 12 mystical names

ORO IBAH AOZPI
MOR DIAL HCTGA
MPH ARSL GAIOL
OIP TEAA PDOCE

The doors of all the temples are now closed and our journey complete.

JEHOVAH TZABAOTH
We thank thee.
Amen

9. LICENCE TO DEPART
The ALPHA and the OMEGA, the beginning and the end, in the spirit of AZOTH. We thank thee, O Mighty Ones, for thy aid. All wisdom gained will be used unselfishly and for the good.
If any spirits be entrapped in this place, pray depart in peace to thy abodes.
May there ever be peace between us.
We thank thee.
Amen

10. QABALISTIC CROSS
Record experiences.

SECTION 2 - THE VISIONS
Each participant had an itemised form on which to record their experiences. Fifty per cent of these were returned. The form itself is featured in Appendix VII.

Part I – VISIONS OF THE WATCHTOWERS
Note: the Watchtowers or Quarters follow the clockwise direction of the compass, namely: East – South – West – North. The Elements follow the descending order detailed in the fourth sub-angle of each Quarter of the Great Table of Earth as described in Dee's diaries: Air – Water – Earth – Fire. Visions from TEX, the Thirtieth Aire, follow in Part II.

The account pools the visions of the Enochian worlds from the travellers. The combined visions build up a fascinating landscape and also include valuable insights from three of the practitioners referred to as Scryers X, Y and Z.

RED WATCHTOWER OF THE EAST

- **GOD NAME OF THE EAST**
  ORO IBAH AOZPI

- **GODS OF THE FOURTH LESSER ANGLE OF THE EAST**
  AOVRRZ (A-O-UR-REZ) to summon
  ALOAI (A-LO-AY) to command

- **ANGELS OF THE ELEMENTS**
  ACCA   Air
  NPAT (EN-PE-AT)   Water
  OTOI (O-TOY)   Earth
  PMOX (P-MOX)   Fire

AIR OF THE EAST

Spring, Daytime, Clear blue sky, Crisp but not cold.
Later, whirling streams of air develop with clouds of white, grey, pale blue.
Flying beings in the air, possibly with wings.
Steep valleys to coast (cf. Norwegian Fjords). Rich grassed slopes, forests, waterfall at head of valley.
Lots of lush greenery, in places seemingly untouched by civilisation of which there was no indication.
Oasis of peacefulness, church or temple on shore.
Two girls with blonde hair chatting happily in cafe on shore.
Angel ACCA: Golden being floating above landscape.
Scryer Y: *A network of signals / communications in the air (the whirling air) reflected on all levels.*
Scryer X: *I knew (either from the Angel [Acca] telling me, or just intuitively) that the flying beings in the sky were a neural network of axons and synapses and that there were signals pinging through the air across the network. It was a model of the physical brain, shown as a network of flying beings in the sky. I was being shown that every thought generates this brain activity and there is immense power in it and it is immensely wasteful to have poor thought control. The angel governs communication and can help me with my communication issues.*

WATER OF THE EAST

Daytime, Clear sky, Equatorial.

Green tumultuous sea – white foam on waves – moving water.

Relates to other forms of running water: rivers, waterfalls, brooks, water spreading across a surface in a pool, and associated sounds, for example, trickling running and falling water.

Galleon on waves.

A flat island. Empty terrain, grass, white sand.

White, functional building containing a temple and a Pool within.

Ancient Egyptian boat (barque?) moored. Keepers (Egyptian) encouraging people to depart in boat.

But Angel NPAT was welcoming and inviting one to stay.

Peaceful, yet powerful control.

Scryer X: *Just images and some information. I can't be sure if I was being told things or if they just came to me from the imagery. "Moving water" was what it was about, which symbolised communication of emotions. Emotions can flow in similar ways to water, which soaks into and permeates things and can take on flavours and mix with other liquids and flavours. Emotion can spread like a cloud and influence an atmosphere just like water can flow, permeate and soak. I was being shown that knowing this gives responsibility to be careful and deliberate in what I give and receive. This is not an interpretation, it's what was being communicated or shown to me.*

EARTH OF THE EAST

Daytime turning to twilight; weather fine and warm.

Deep forest, tropical, large leaves, dark green, humid but visible against the sky and reflected in any water present, such as pools and rivers. Setting sun reflected in shiny leaves, shining yellow on the water, Ahead there is the whirling sky and frothing ocean of the air and water elements.

Powerful elemental forces.

Cultivated garden area.

A Fawn, crocodile, and dragons spotted.

Egyptian beings.

Angel OTOI: presence detected.

Scryer Z: *The angel gave off feminine vibrations to begin with, then gave off sharper more masculine vibrations which felt fierce at times – but despite this felt friendly throughout, basically giving me a guided tour of the garden.*
Forces – powerful, restless and active.
Inland from the forest the terrain is red, dry, arid and mountainous. Wind strong and noisy, the earth churned and flung into air.
Scryer X: *The Earth was restless and driven, determined; hence thrust up into the air. It felt powerful, yet bullish, pushing aside obstacles. I was being shown that this restless, driven Earth was Will – active and powerful.*

FIRE OF THE EAST

Daytime, very hot, bright
Desert landscape with large, white crystals glowing with fire.
Beneath is vast underground lava filled cavern. Extremely hot.
Dark red fires, warming, - causing the water to evaporate to the air.
Scryer Y: *The fire is under the other elements, powering them, giving them movement, life, a cyclic process. The fire arouses an awakening, the creativity of life, a basic sexuality which must not be denied. Important not to repress desire.*
Angel PMOX: *glowing, vibrant, magnetic, charismatic, instructive, educative.*
Scryer Z: *Slight sense of the angel's presence.*
Scryer X: *PMOX appeared immediately, aglow and vibrant. Handsome, charismatic, positively electric. Great personal magnetism. Very cheeky (kept doing these double eyebrow-raises, as if to create innuendo in everything he said). He was fascinating and I felt drawn to him.*
I had a vision within the vision (i.e. like a daydream or reverie, or maybe like he was showing me something) of him somehow causing my Kundalini to awaken, afire, and shoot up, blowing my mind. It made me feel powerful and creative. I wanted to create. I wanted to have sex. . It was a feeling of wanting to, but it was not directed towards any particular person. He was telling me of the importance and power of sexual magnetism. It is a reservoir of power to create or heal or do whatever you will. It was clear he enjoyed and encouraged sex but somehow this was not crass or uncomfortable. He was encouraging me to use my sexual virility and not suppress it, but treat it as a sacred and powerful force.

WHITE WATCHTOWER OF THE SOUTH
- GOD NAME OF THE SOUTH
  MOR DIAL HCTGA

- GODS OF THE FOURTH LESSER ANGLE OF THE SOUTH
  SPMNIR (ESPE – EMNIR) to summon
  ILPIZ to command

- ANGELS OF THE ELEMENTS
  MSAL (EM - SAL) Air
  IABA (YABA) Water
  IZXP (IZ - EX – PE) Earth
  STIM (ES – TEEM) Fire

AIR OF THE SOUTH

Daytime, flat grassed landscape.

A tornado whirling back and forth.

Originally (or later the wind becomes) a loud, strong, biting and driving high wind above cities, mountains, plains, icy wastes and subterranean terrain, where stalactites of glowing crystal are growing.

Scryer Y: *The wind becomes an endless whirl, an unchallenged execution of the Will resulting in positive creation.*

Angel MSAL: presence detected, white, yellow, grey bearded.

Scryer X: *I was being instructed that this was the swift, decisive, executive aspect of the action of thought. It is creation, the full-stop at the end of a process of thought, that results in action. Creation. Also, the dividing up and measuring of time. Clear focus, then execution of Will.*

WATER OF THE SOUTH

Endless calm deep, dark blue sea, mirror like surface.

Golden, orange setting sun on left-hand.

Sense marine life below in sea.

Journey on barque towards setting sun.

Scryer Y: *But beneath the calm is the power of water and its driving force channelled beneficially, physically and spiritually.*

Scryer X: *I was not shown a landscape but fleeting images of powerful water- waterfalls, hydro-turbines, stinging rain and water balloons. Feeling of a powerful force, with strong inertia. Like a wall of water, but more focussed. I was being shown that this is the focussed emotional force, channelled and directed. Very powerful. Emotional control is required in the sense of understanding the nature of such forces and how to summon, direct focus and channel them, rather than control in the sense of suppressing one's emotions.*

EARTH OF THE SOUTH

Daytime.
Arrival on land in barque from sea journey from the Water of the South.
Disembark, not to look back.
Flat, endless, red, stony desert.
Then its opposite: black soil under icecap.
A camel with deep dark eyes transported its rider like the wind across the desert.
Constant, unchanging.

Scryer Y: *The power of earthquakes, landslides, physical laws and man's application, and on a universal level, the gravitational power of celestial bodies.*

Scryer X: *Once again, not so much a landscape as a series of images. Images of a powerful, destructive Earth- earthquakes, landslides, etc. Also, it was as though I was being shown physics laws and their applications, in particular gravity. Images of planets, weights and pulleys, magnetism, heavy things being lifted, pushed and pulled by ropes, etc.*

I was told that these forces and laws do not change and you must work with them. The laws are fixed but what our human minds project onto them and how we see and interpret them can be changed though, they are open to interpretation if you don't break the fundamental laws. I got the impression there was some important magical and psychological secret in these things, but I couldn't quite grasp it. It made more sense at the time than it does reading it back now!

FIRE OF THE SOUTH

Daytime
Hot burning plains/desert. Myriads of flames like grass across terrain.

Then Electric storms, sparks, lightening but nothing enduring.
Burning buildings, but no heat nor destruction.
A furnace with hot glowing coals with 4 workers.
Angel STIM: White-haired and elderly.

Scryer Z: *One of the furnace workers pointed me towards the furnace, both he and STIM told me to eat one of the coals for more energy — so, friendliness and helpfulness.*
He and one worker offer hot coal to eat for energy.

Scryer Y: *The fire in this quarter is purifying and inspirational. Fire purifies the other elements, purges, renews. A journey has commenced.*

Scryer X: *The commentary or instruction that went with this was pretty traditional Hermetic instruction on the element of Fire. It is a spark but it doesn't endure, yet it is of principal importance in setting the tone of an operation- like the light-bulb moment of an idea that sparks and fades, yet inspires the work. Fire also destroys, yet it is a purge of the outdated and old, to make way for the new.*

GREEN WATCHTOWER OF THE WEST

- GOD NAME OF THE WEST
  MPH ARSL GAIOL

- GODS OF THE FOURTH LESSER ANGLE OF THE WEST
  IAAASD (YA –A – ASDE) to summon
  ATAPA to command

- ANGELS OF THE ELEMENTS
  XPEN (EX - PEN) Air
  VASA Water
  DAPI Earth
  RNIL (UR - NEEL) Fire

AIR OF THE WEST

Late Summer or Autumn.
Day, dark stormy clouds, endlessly tumbling.
  Humid, stifling, still about to rain.
  Lush green valley and waterfall at head (cf Air of East).

Mushrooms, bird still singing.
Peaceful and meditative and receptive; friendliness and helpfulness.
Vision of faery folk, friendly and helpful, also cat-like Egyptian female.
Rise above the storm into clear air, higher and higher until on brink of Water World of the West.

Scryer X: *Peaceful, meditative feeling. I have written "Air of the West" is a place to go to meditate, to create the right state for receptive meditation. Again, this stuff just came to be rather than me analysing things: the humid air is heavy with water, as though pregnant; Air is thought and water is the unconscious; the atmosphere is analogous to the mental state when meditating, particularly meditation that is to receive something; the mind is still and receptive.*

WATER OF THE WEST

Daytime, fine weather.
There is an island in an endless sea of deep still water (the unconscious?)
Temple on an island. Perhaps the same as one in Eastern water World. A long narrow pool runs through it, narrowing and widening as passes through separate sections of the temple.
Female angels with vases of healing water in each section.
Vision of the cat-like Egyptian female.
From the sea is a river running through woodland. Follow river to a waterfall and then on to its source. Becomes a stream, then a rivulet in rocky ground.
Higher and higher to the meeting of the Air of the West.

Scryer X: *Whilst the Air of the West described the meditative state, Water of the West described the "stuff" of the unconscious itself. Stillness was the important message.*

EARTH OF THE WEST

Night, Cold.
Woodland, grass.
Friendly wolf, howling.
Seeds in the wet earth, incubating, growing, life. Receptive, feminine watery soil "impregnated" by the seed and it incubates in the womb-like soil and grows into life.

Seeds in the unconscious, source of ideas.

The perpetuation of Nature.

The Subterranean world descends to rocky caves and a deep hole to cavern at base.

Lizards on side of hole.

Large lizard in cavern – the king or Queen?

Scryer X: *There was more commentary than visuals- the soil and seed was obviously symbolic of sexual forces in nature. Whilst the imagery wasn't sexual, symbolically it was and it really felt sexual. In another sense, seeds (male) are planted in the unconscious (female), impregnating it, and it bears fruit in the conscious mind eventually. This is also sexual, but on a different, non-physical level.*

FIRE OF THE WEST

Sunset. Or at least, the light looked like it. A world in which it is perpetually sunset.

Terrain of all the minerals and their spirits (helpful).

Spirits of the minerals. Strange creatures of the night are coming in the air, fluttering above.

Below ground, there are fire bursts and explosions. Lizards become salamanders, living in the fire.

Fire invigorates the other elements – a volcanic movement through the elemental layers above: earth, water, air.

Scryer X: *Atmosphere and lighting is eerie and ominous. The "things of the night" are near, are coming, and you wonder if you already see them flittering at the edge of your vision but you can't fix on them. Everything feels as though it's about to "check-out", fade away, as though near-death, or heading towards the world of the dead in the East, the sunset. The sun obviously has this feeling too, because that is exactly what it is doing, in the old sun-dies-every-night world-view.*

I got the impression that the message was about recognising when something has run its course and its time has come. Not holding on to outmoded/dead things. I suspect this is an interpretation rather than something I was told, but I can't be certain now.

Scryer Y: *Atmosphere is eerie and slightly foreboding. Everything is going towards the sunset, a downward spiral, the dying before regeneration. An awareness of the finiteness of everything.*

BLACK (BILBERRY) WATCHTOWER OF THE NORTH
- GOD NAME OF THE NORTH
  OIP TEAA PDOCE

- GODS OF THE FOURTH LESSER ANGLE OF THE NORTH
  RZIONR (URZI – ONUR) to summon
  NRZFM (NUR – ZEFM) to command

- ANGELS OF THE ELEMENTS
  ADRE   Air
  SISP (SIS – PE)   Water
  PALI   Earth
  ACAR   Fire

AIR OF THE NORTH
Winter, dark possibly night. High above clouds travelling.
Scryer Z: *I come through the air to a gold sphere and into a sphere inside that sphere, where I was shown a book of wisdom with my name on it.*
Here is a personalised Book of Wisdom (contents undisclosed).
Beings present, including the Angel ADRE and other non-human beings inside the inner sphere.
Scryer Z: *ADRE is my guide to the spheres.*
All are helpful.
Vision: Magi celebrating around a table in a candlelit cavern with firelight and shadows.
A very special place to communicate.
Scryer X: *Vision took place very high up above the clouds. For some reason I got the impression (whether told or otherwise) that this was a place of communication, in Briah, to which you could ascend in order to communicate with ascended, deceased or others that have ascended (like yourself, if there).*
Scryer Y: *Below the ground, air beneath the earth rushes through endless tunnels and caverns, invigorating the whole planet. The elements interconnect, performing*

functions, which take them across the whole globe.
BUT THEY ORIGINATE HERE IN THE NORTH.

WATER OF THE NORTH

Daytime

A black still ocean; then an enormous wave.

A ship on the crest of the wave.

Inside is a room with tanks of large goldfish with water constantly humming and bubbling through filters, which in a way organises the wildness of the wave.

Then a huge Marlin diving up and down,

Connect to this creature and rush across oceans.

Scryer X: *I have the following written, and I'm unsure if it was my interpretation or something I was told:*

"On Earth in human form, our consciousness is compartmentalised and separated from others in order to sustain life and keep us sane. The filter is filtering this experience to fit the way we perceive things, so it doesn't freak us out."

Vision: Magi still celebrating in the candlelit cavern.

EARTH OF THE NORTH

Winter, dark and dank.

Fierce, but friendly, dogs are about and mythical creatures.

Scryer X: *I saw various mythical creatures- Ents, dryads, nymphs, etc., some from known mythological sources such as the "Vainamoinon" (from the Finnish "Kalevala") and some from "Lord of the Rings". And a "solar-phallic Pan" (as I have written in my notes, rather than just "Pan"?) was also there and he was having his way with the nymphs and dryads and fertilises the earth.*

Scryer Y: *Beneath are dark subterranean tunnels in the earth.*

Emerge (reborn from Pan's seed?) from tunnels, floating high in the air, looking over beautiful landscape. The whole land is invigorated by Northern Air beneath. Pyramids and palm trees in distance.

Scryer X: *A strong environmental "vibe" was felt also, as though this realm is precious and shouldn't be spoiled.*

FIRE OF THE NORTH
Autumn, Daytime

But for **Scryer X**: *The sky was red-tinged and it coloured everything in view- it looked like everything was under a fiery sunset, yet also a bit blurred and surreal. A forest of American pine and sparsely-leaved trees. The latter had shed most of their leaves. There was a thin covering of brownish-red leaves on ground.*

Scryer Z: *Somewhere the forest is burning. Fire is needed to destroy the old vegetation to allow new growth.*

The beautiful landscape of the Earth of the North is now consumed by flames fed by the Air of the North beneath. Fire crackling as timber burnt; the smell of smoke.

Scryer X: *There was a beautiful woman lying on the ground with flower petals on the ground in an around her auburn hair, which was strewn across the ground around her head.*

Now a red tinged sky, colouring all, blurred and surreal, by the fires, plus the advent of a fiery sunset

Scryer Z: *Vision of the Goddess Gaia,*[78] *the Earth in mother or crone aspect*

Scryer X: *My vision of the petal-strewn, erotically naked woman is no doubt the young, fecund, alter-ego of the crone. The woman beckoned to me, wanting me to "have her". We had sex and our climactic cry seemed to echo across the universe. The earth was fertilised beneath us as a result and burst to life.*[79] *She laid back down in the same pose as when I discovered her and I knew this would repeat itself for as long as I was able to stay and I knew that I could and would.*

The sexual fulfilment of Gaia gives birth to Uranus, the Heavens. Simultaneously, the earth is fertilised, regenerated and springs into life after the fiery imagery witnessed by all travellers.

And so the scryers move onwards to TEX, THE THIRTIETH AIRE.

---

78. Gaia is the ancestral mother of all life, the primal Mother Earth. She gave birth to Uranus, the sky or heaven.

Part II – VISIONS OF TEX, THE THIRTIETH AIRE

THE FOUR ANGELIC KINGS

The Angelic Kings are responsible for guiding from place to place, safety, advancement, vision of spiritual progress.

ARFAOLG (AR- FA – OLDG)
ZARNAAH (ZAR – NA – AH)
HONONOL (HO-NO – NOL)
ZURCHOL (ZU- RE – KOL)

Day and night.
Cloudy, misty and dull.
Cold and dank like late Autumn or Winter.
Green mountains, forested with pine.
Stags in the forest.
Grey gorge or ravine with river at the bottom, forest path and a stone bridge, which later collapsed (see below)
Life forms encountered include:
Silver dragon.
Two birds.
Warthog (Zurchol).
Human being (Hononol).
Ghostly rider and horse (Arfaolg and Zarnaah?)

Scryer X: *The angel ZURCHOL appeared in the form of a warthog, not unlike the "Hakuna Matata" singing character from the "Lion King". I thought this was a bit silly so I said the four names of the Kings again and he remained and insisted he was He.*

HONONEL was introduced after ZURCHOL, but I haven't written down anything about his appearance. From memory he was in a plain-clothes human form.

Scryer Y: *The birds revealed a house high-up the cliff-face of a ravine. I went inside and a tunnel led to the top of the cliff where there was a pagan temple of stones. The Sun was high in the clear blue sky overhead. I became aware of the endless layers of the Aires above and the seemingly Infinite beyond. Below was the cloud-shrouded planet.*

Scryer Z: *A silver dragon guided me to and from a golden pyramid with a golden book inside (contents undisclosed).*

At night, the ghostly rider had to rescue Scryer X from the river, after the bridge collapsed, and together they rode high over the cliffs to a clearing with a fire [was this another dimension of the temple visited by Scryer Y?]. The warthog and the human were present. Both delivered insightful advice. Here is the account from

Scryer X.*I walked along a forest path, seeing a stag, then the path turned left and I came to the cliff and proceeded to cross the ravine via the stone bridge. It broke and I fell a long way down into the water. Very cold. Went downstream a bit and saw a ghostly horse and rider running in the air near the bank to my right. I grabbed on and it took me way up, above the cliffs.*

I zoned out a few times, quite exhausted from the long day, nearly falling asleep. Landed in a clearing with a campfire and the warthog character (Zurchol). Used the king names to test the spirit and he stayed. He told me to tell him any troubles and he would try to help. I told him some relationship stuff and what he said was insightful and, with a month of hindsight, a little prophetic. He said HONONEL could help me with initiatory-path-related questions. He described my point in my initiatory career fairly well.

I nearly nodded off again.

Then we were called back and I retraced my steps to the forest path on which I started.

With the passing of the Æthyrs, the Angelic worlds and The Divine now await

17. Gustave Doré. *Empyrean,* Dante's *Divina Commedia: Paradiso,* canto XXXI, 1868. [80]

80. Public domain via Wikipedia Commons

PART THREE

APPENDICES

APPENDIX I
ALEISTER CROWLEY AND
ENOCHIAN MAGIC

An abridged transcript of a talk by Robin E. Cousins for the *Aleister Crowley Conference*, Saturday 13 September 2014, Clun, Shropshire, organised by the Pagan Federation Mid Wales and West.[81]

The worldwide interest in Enochian or Angelic Magic can be credited directly to Aleister Crowley. He followed the system developed by the Hermetic Order of the Golden Dawn, which had been founded by William Wynn Westcott (1848-1925), Samuel Liddell MacGregor Mathers (1854-1918) and William Robert Woodman (1828-1891) in London in 1887. Most students of the magical arts only became aware of Enochian Magic through the writings of Crowley and Israel Regardie, his secretary from 1928 until 1932, who had published various Golden Dawn papers between 1937 and 1940.

Nevertheless, not everyone practises the same version of Enochian as the followers of Crowley and the Golden Dawn. The Enochian system of angel magic originated and developed from the angelic conversations of John Dee and Edward Kelley during the late sixteenth century. They never used the term "Enochian" to describe it. The system remained in obscurity until the early twentieth century. This was largely because information was not generally available until then. Dee's magical diaries existed only in manuscript form in the Library at the British Museum in Bloomsbury (it became part of the British Library in 1973), which few were able to access.[82]

The exception was the section of diaries published in 1659 by Meric Casaubon as *A True and Faithful Relation of what passed between Dr Dee and some Spirits*, but this was soon out-of-print and remained as such until the late twentieth century.

However, during the 1670s, it would appear various unidentified magicians

---

81. The transcript (with additional footnotes) has been abridged in order to avoid the duplication of sections of the main text, although some repetition was unavoidable.
82. In 1997, the British Library moved to new premises in Euston.

worked with Dee and Kelley's angel magic. Using Casaubon's *A True and Faithful Relation* as the main source, a system was formulated concentrating on the Great Table of Earth. Details of its construction were expanded and extensive invocations added, resulting in the creation of a practical Enochian grimoire or Book of Spirits. The authorship of the manual is not known, but at least four manuscript copies are known to have been made. These manuscripts are now published in *Practical Angel Magick of Dr John Dee's Enochian Tables*, edited by Stephen Skinner and David Rankine. See the Bibliography for full details.

One of these, now British Library Sloane MS 307, which some scholars believe to be the original workbook, was used by the Golden Dawn for their Enochian teachings,

Owing to the dependence on *A True and Faithful Relation*, many of that book's errors (usually involving angel names) are repeated in the workbook and the subsequent copies, thereby betraying their common source and proving that Dee's original manuscripts were not consulted, despite some mistakenly believing they were. One example is Crowley's Saharan demon Choronzon.[83] His name is spelt "*Coronzom*" in the diaries, but "*Coronzon*" in *A True and Faithful Relation*. Sloane MS 307 more or less completely copies the relevant paragraph from *A True and Faithful Relation*, but Coronzon is now spelt "***Ch****oronzon*". Crowley popularised this version, perhaps possibly unaware of the original diary spelling.

Westcott adapted Sloane MS 307 to create a system of Enochian Magic known as *Book H* or *Clavicula Tabularum Enoch* for an inner order of the Golden Dawn, called the Red Rose and the Golden Cross, which had become active in 1892 and incorporated the grades: Adeptus Minor, Adeptus Major and Adeptus Exemptus. With Mather's help, Westcott expanded and complicated the original system of Dee and Kelley, altering its basic structure.

It was this Golden Dawn version of Enochian that Crowley promoted and made available when he published *LIBER CHANOKH Sub Figurâ LXXXIV- A Brief Abstract of the Symbolic Representation of the Universe derived by Doctor John Dee through the Skrying of Sir Edward Kelley* in his periodical *THE EQUINOX*, Volume 1, nos. 7 and 8 in 1912.[84]

Crowley had also published in *THE EQUINOX* the previous year (Vol.1, no.5, 1911) *The Vision and the Voice (Liber 418)* – his account of scrying in the Enochian

---

83. T&FR, p92; for the original diary entry, see British Library MS Cotton Appendix XLVI, Part I, fol.92r. 84. Chanokh is an old Hebrew form of Enoch.

spirit world of the Thirty Aires or Æthyrs that surround the terrestrial world.

When Israel Regardie published the Golden Dawn papers between 1937 and 1940 he included a detailed introduction to the Golden Dawn version of the angelic tablets, including the 48 angelic calls or keys, but not *Book H*. Until more Enochian publications appeared in recent years, Crowley and Regardie's writings were the only sources of information on the system generally available, otherwise it meant a trip to the British Museum.

Crowley was impressed by Kelley and regarded Dee as hardly better than Kelley's secretary.

"*I suspected Kelley of finding Dee unsupportable at times with his pity, pedantry, credulity, respectability and lack of humour*". [85]

Of Kelley, Crowley wrote:

"*To condemn Kelley as a cheating charlatan – the accepted view – is simply stupid. If he invented Enochian and composed the superb prose, he was at worst a Chatterton with fifty times that poet's ingenuity and five hundred times his poetical genius. I prefer to judge Kelley from this, rather than from the stale scandal of people, to whom any magician smelt of sulphur.*" [86]

In fact, Crowley, after spiritually exploring past lives, considered himself to be a reincarnation of Kelley or, as he preferred to say – Kelley was his precarnation, along with other infamous celebrities, such as: Cagliostro, Eliphas Levi, and Pope Alexander VI allegedly a black magician, whose name was used to preface such Höllenzwänge or so-called Faustian hell-books, as the *Geister Commando* [The Command of Spirits]. To understand the Golden Dawn Enochian system to which Crowley was committed, a brief history of Angelic or Enochian Magic now follows from which it is possible to glean why Crowley was so impressed by Kelley.

It was Kelley who taught Dee the techniques of magic when he arrived in Mortlake in March 1582. He was an experienced magician. In Krakow in 1584, Kelley revealed, that assisted by a Dr or Mr Myniver (of whom nothing is known), he had once summoned a wicked spirit Sendenna or Sondenna, which had appeared in a Triangle of Fire. The spirit (which had taken the form of a "great Gyant") was constrained and was supposed to reveal names of various spirits and their offices perhaps for a system of magic.[87] Thirty-four years after Kelley's death, the antiquarian John Weever (1576-1632) wrote in his *Ancient Funerall Monuments*

---

85. *The Confessions*, p. 665. 86. Ibid., p.664. Thomas Chatterton(1752-1770) forged medieval poetry which was severely criticised and he committed suicide with arsenic at the age of 17. 87. *T&FR*, p.185. "Soudenna" is the original diary version; see British Library MS Cotton Appendix XLVI, Part I, fol.201v.

(1631) about Kelley practising necromancy with a certain Paul Waring in the churchyard of St Leonard's church, Walton-le-Dale, near Preston, Lancashire. Further details on this story can be found in Appendix VI.

John Dee was *"desyrous to haue help in my philosophicall studies throwgh the cumpany and information of the blessed angels of god."* [88] All the usual means of study had failed. So Dee attempted to make contact with those "angels of god". But he was rubbish at scrying. He had tried since 1579, assisted by various useless scryers, to obtain

"Such wisdom, as I might know the nature of god's creatures; and also the means to use them to his honour and glory". [89]

Over a few months Kelley revolutionised Dee's magical dabbling and through Kelley's scrying, the Enochian system began to develop. It included:

1. The Seal of God or Truth — *Sigillum Dei Æmæth* that was placed under the crystal on the Holy Table to attract spiritual forces. This was surrounded by the seven talismans known as the *Ensigns Of Creation*. Kelley had obviously encountered similar Seals of God. They were well known, for obtaining visions of the "true and living God". See Chapter One for more details.

2. A complete system of angelic magic, called the *Heptarchia Mystica*, for the seven traditional planets and the days of the week. All the angels feature on the Seal of God. Dee and Kelley were frequently in contact with the Heptarchian angels when they were in Krakow.

3. The Angelic or Enochian Alphabet of the Holy Language spoken by God and the angels. The prophet Enoch, who was "taken" by God and had conversed in the Angelic Tongue, wrote the divine secrets in his book, now lost.

4. *Liber Loagaeth* aka *The Book of the Speech from God*, which included 48 tables of alphabetic squares over 96 sides There are 2,401 squares per side and the book, which had been magically transmitted to Kelley, was supposedly the lost *Book of Enoch* itself.

5. Forty-Eight Angelic Keys or Calls derived from *Liber Loagaeth*. These are a series of invocations, of which thirty are designed to open the Thirty Aires or Æthyrs or Heavens (each with three Angelic Kings) surrounding the Terrestrial

---

88. Peterson, Joseph, ed. *John Dee's Five Books of Mysteries*, p.66.
89. *T&FR*, p. 231.

World of the Four Quarters or Watchtowers, aka the Great Table of Earth

6. The Great Table of Earth is derived from Kelley's *Vision of the Four Castles* describing the 4 quarters thus: East - "Fresh Red Cullor"; South - "Lilly White"; West –"dark Greene Cullor like garlicke blades" ; North – "Blacke as of Bilbery Juyce". The quarters are held together by the Black Cross or Cross of Union. Each quarter is divided into four Sub-Angles with different functions. One sub-angle in each quarter dealt with the Knowledge and Use of the Four Elements, with an angel for each element so there was no need to assign elements to the quarters as the Golden Dawn did.

John Dee tabulated the names and functions of all the gods and angels of the

18. Kelley and Paul Waring at Walton-Le-Dale, from Ebenezer Sibly's 'A New and Complete Illustration of the Occult Sciences', 1806.

Four Quarters or Watchtowers derived from the Great Table and wrote invocations in the *Book of Supplications and Invocations*. Some scholars believe this to be the actual *Book of Enoch*.

Kelley's genius shines with the creation of the Angelic Calls or Keys. The Calls were laboriously extracted in Enochian from the tables of the *Liber Loagaeth*, letter by letter, backwards from the end of each Call. Later the angels provided translations from which our knowledge of Enochian derives. Considering the Calls were delivered backwards and rapidly, the translation is consistent, even though the vocabulary is somewhat limited. Whether the system was the direct result of Kelley's scrying or from his past experience (maybe with the mysterious Dr Myniver), at some point the system must have been divinely inspired.

On 20 April 1587, while Dee, Kelley and their families were staying with Count Vilém z Rožmberk, the Vice Regent of Bohemia, (1535-92) at his castle in Třeboň in South Bohemia, Kelley received a revised version of the Great Table of Earth known as the Table of Raphael.

19. Třeboň medieval fortications. (Photograph © R.E. Cousins)

It was delivered by the Angel Raphael, after whom it has been named. The new table changes some letters and switches the positions of some of the quarters. It also threw a spanner into the works, as Dee's *Book of Supplications* no longer tallied with the new Table. However, the validity of the new arrangement is suspect and it seems inextricably entangled with the wife-swapping arrangement between Dee and Kelley. At this time, Kelley's reputation regarding his alchemical and metallurgical skills had grown. He had received quite lucrative offers from Rožmberk and his brother Petr Vok Rožmberk (1539-1611) for reviving Bohemian gold mines and demonstrating alchemical skills.

Kelley now wished to be free of the partnership with Dee. Apparently, he had prayed all Lent that he could be released (4 April 1587).

1. It would seem that Kelley devised the notorious wife swapping sessions in order to extract himself from the actions, but he shot himself in the foot as he did not expect Dee to agree.

2. Kelley had said that the swop was part of the procedure to obtain new divine secrets. The revised great table may have been devised as "new wisdom" to give weight to Kelley's plan.

3. Unfortunately for Kelley, Dee being desperate for knowledge, readily agreed to the swap, especially as it appeared to have "Divine Approval". Believing it to be God's will, Dee felt it was the only way to receive the secrets desired. He was told by the Angels – "Not to prefer your Reason before the wisdom of the Highest". He was entrapped. He was utterly resolved to obey the new doctrine and on 3rd May

20. The Black Cross rearranged as the Tablet of Union

1587 the Pact was sealed whereby the four

> ... covenanted with god, and subscribed the same, for indissoluble and inviolable unities, charity and friendship keeping between us four, and all things between us in common... [90]

The so-called Act of Obedience or the exchange of wives took place on 22 May 1587. The day after, Dee asked obsequiously if, "*we might be instructed in the understanding and practice of Wisdom ... what the Almighty God shall deem meet for us to know.*" [91]

He hoped in vain, for all that happened was that Jane Dee gave birth to Theodore (which means "God-given") virtually nine months later on 28 February 1588. Was he Kelley's child? The Dee and Kelley partnership was was finished. No more information was received regarding the Angelic system. The "Gift of God" died, aged three, in Spring 1601 in Manchester.

However, the Enochian system used by the Crowley and the Golden Dawn is not the same as the one originally delivered to Dee and Kelley. This is what happened.

The anonymous magician(s) who created the practical Enochian system detailed in Sloane MS 307 used the revised Great Table of Raphael. They also dispensed with the Black Cross of Union holding the 4 quarters of the Earth together. The 4 names on the cross were reorganised into a small tablet known as the "Tablet of Union" that was placed in the centre of the Four Quarters or Watchtowers. Dee had actually noted the four names down in this format (see *T&FR*, p.179), but as a small tablet it was never incorporated into the design of Dee and Kelley's Great Table of Earth, as it is in Sloane MS 307.

No more is heard until Westcott devised the Golden Dawn Enochian system from Sloane MS 307 for the Adeptus Minor grade of the Order, though it would seem not many people knew much about it. However, this did not apply to Crowley, who had joined the Order in 1898. He actively practised and promoted the Golden Dawn Enochian system. Westcott, a Coroner, left the Order in 1896/7 after he had compromised his job by leaving Golden Dawn papers in a Hansom Cab. Mathers was now in control and the inevitable personality clashes led to his authority being challenged. Crowley quickly worked his way up, deliberately befriending the unpopular Mathers. Much to the disapproval of the rest of the Order, Crowley was

90. *T&FR*, p *21. 91. Ibid., p.*24.

initiated as Adeptus Minor by Mathers in Paris in January 1900, thereby gaining access to Enochian material.

In the Golden Dawn system, the directional quarters making up the 4 Watchtowers of the Physical World became the Four Elements of the terrestrial world. They follow the traditional associations and colouring, as follows:

EAST – AIR –Yellow with Amethyst lettering
WEST – WATER – Blue with Orange lettering
SOUTH – FIRE – Red with Green lettering
NORTH – EARTH – Black with White lettering
CENTRE – SPIRIT – White with Black lettering

The original 4 subdivisions of each quarter now became elemental sub-angles. For example, the Eastern Quarter became the Air Tablet and its four sub angles were renamed Air of Air; Water of Air; Fire of Air; and Earth of Air. The Tablet of Union was now attributed to The Spirit.

As Sloane MS 307 was derived purely from Dee's diaries as printed in *A True and Faithful Relation*, much of the original system was missing, since the remaining magical diaries had yet to be discovered when the book was published. The Golden Dawn's Book *H*, which in turn stems from Sloane MS 307, therefore, also lacks these features. Moreover, other sections were deliberately excluded. These were not included in the Golden Dawn Enochian writings that Israel Regardie published and from which he also omitted *Book H*.

Items excluded are:
- Magician's ring and lamen.
- Use of the Holy Table and *Sigillum Dei* (Seal of God).
- *Heptarchia Mystica* the system of planetary magic.
- *The Liber Loagaeth*.
- List of the functions of the angels (These were deliberately excluded as they are present in *Book H*).
- *Book of Supplication and Invocations*.
- The Thirty Aires or Æthyrs that Crowley explored himself, but which were barely mentioned by the Golden Dawn.
- Kelley's *Vision of the Four Castles* which gave rise to the Great Table and was later reproduced as a gold talisman, now in the British Museum.

Crowley, of course, was not content with the incomplete system. His *Liber Chanokh SubFigurâ LXXXIV - A Brief Abstract of the Symbolic Representation of the Universe derived by Doctor John Dee through the scrying of Sir Edward Kell[e]y* has the following "Preparatory Note by the Editor" [i.e., Crowley], emphasizing the missing features.

"We omit in this preliminary sketch any account of the *Tables of Soyga*, *The Heptarchia Mystica*, *The Book of Enoch*, or *Liber Loagaeth*. We hope to be able to deal with these adequately in a subsequent article", but unfortunately this never materialised. He wrote:

"It was part of my plan for The Equinox to prepare a final edition of the work of Dr Dee and Sir Edward Kelley. I had a good many of the data and promised myself to complete them by studying the manuscripts in the Bodleian."[92]

Crowley did study the manuscripts but nothing was ever published. However, unlike *Book H* and Regardie's Golden Dawn writings, the Brief Abstract did include

- Diagrams of the *Sigillum Dei* and the Holy Table,
- Brief information on the Heptarchian angels featured on the Seal.
- A listing of the Thirty Aires or Æthyrs with their Angelic Kings

Crowley was in favour of the additions Westcott and Mathers made to what were now the Enochian Elemental Tablets. They made the system extremely complicated in the following ways.

- Enochian letters were added to the squares – these were never on the Dee and Kelley original, which contained only Latin letters.
- Each little square was turned into a truncated pyramid.
- The flat top of the pyramid displays the letter
- The four sides of the pyramids have various correspondences, including the Sephiroth of the Qabalistic Tree of Life, the Planets, the Elements and Zodiacal signs. By using these, this in turn led to the associated Tarot card, Geomantic sign and Hebrew letter also being assigned, along with their appropriate colours.

With all these colours being inserted on the tablets, multicoloured pyramids now resulted making the Great Table look like a mismanaged artist's palette.

Further additions caused an increase in the number of angels on the tablets

- With the original Dee system, each Quarter has a total of 32 angels controlled by 12 Lesser Gods (their immediate superiors).

---

92. *The Confessions*, p.645.

- The Golden Dawn elemental equivalent quarter has 80 angels with 80 Archangels (as the Lesser Gods are now called) as their immediate superiors.

They also introduced a complicated system for pronouncing Enochian which was completely unnecessary as Dee's instructions were in *T&FR*. Dee broke words into syllables similar to English, but sometimes pronounced letters individually. The Golden Dawn pronunciation was based on the Hebrew vowel system to deal with consonant clusters, resulting in every letter being pronounced, making it very awkward and unwieldy at times.

Crowley soon began investigating the system in greater depth, including the use of the Angelic Keys or Calls and the Thirty Aires or Æthyrs surrounding the material world, which the Golden Dawn had ignored:

> "The genuiness of these keys, altogether apart from any critical observation, is guaranteed by the fact that anyone with the smallest capacity for Magic finds that they work."[93]

In July 1900, he went to Mexico where he painted the four elemental Watchtowers and began to scry the Aires. There are 48 Calls altogether – the first 18 the Golden Dawn assigned to the Great Table of Earth for opening the four elemental tablets, although there is no mention of this use in Dee's diaries. The remaining thirty are to open the Aires, which Dee's diaries do instruct. The thirty Calls are basically the same call (no. 19) with just the name of the Aire changed to differentiate. When Crowley employed them, he referred to them as the "Cry of the Æthyrs". As we have seen in Chapter Two, the Aires are dominions extending in ever widening circles without and beyond the watchtowers of the universe. The closest Aire to the Earth is the Thirtieth (TEX), which appears to form an etheric veil around the planet. The First Aire (LIL) borders the super celestial world of the angels and archangels

In Mexico, however, Crowley found that even he did not have enough experience of Enochian yet. After scrying the first two Aires – number 30 (TEX) and number 29 (RII) he abandoned the experiment.

> "In Mexico I thought I would discover for myself what the Æthyrs really were, by working them in turn by means of the 19th Key and scrying in the spirit vision... I investigated the first two on November 14th and 17th 1900. The 'vision and the

---

93. *The Confessions*, p.665. 94. *The Confessions*, p.665.

voice' was mysterious and terrific in character. What I saw was not beyond my previous experience, but what I heard was as unintelligible to me as [William] Blake to a Baptist. I found that I could no more force myself to go on to the 28th Æthyr, than I could throw myself from a cliff".[94]

Nevertheless, he preserved the magical record and had no thoughts of continuing for nine years,

He had left Mexico in 1902, eventually arriving back in the UK in 1903. In 1904 he published *The Goetia*, the first book of the *Lemegeton* or *Lesser key of Solomon*, which had been translated by Mathers. Editing this with many vicious comments, he kept the Enochian flag flying by pointlessly rendering all the conjurations in the Angelic Language, using the Angelic Calls or keys as his dictionary. By the time of the reception of the *Book of Law (Liber AL vel Legis, sub figura CCXX)* in Cairo, 8-10th April 1904, Enochian was part of his regular magical routine.

For example, from his *The Record of the Magical Retirement (John St John)* in October 1908, he wrote:

"I shall rise and chant the Enochian calls and invoke the Bornless One, and clear a few of the devils away, and get an army of mighty angels around me."

Crowley had turned his back on the Golden Dawn and Mathers. In 1907, he had formed his Order of the Silver Star (Argenteum Astrum) to replace the Golden Dawn, which irritated his former friend. The knife was twisted when in the second issue of *The Equinox* (September 1909), Crowley published some of the Golden Dawn rituals. An injunction by Mathers failed.

Crowley managed to lose the Enochian tablets he painted in Mexico. He thought they were in Boleskine, but failed to find them and, after putting Victor Neuburg through his initiation, including having him sleep naked on a bed of gorse for a week, returned to London, where he found the tablets in his loft under skis. To his delight, lurking beneath the tablets was his manuscript of the *Book of Law(Liber AL vel Legis, sub figura CCXX)*, which had also been lost for some time.

He resumed his work with the Æthyrs while on a trek through the Algerian Sahara with Victor Neuburg in late 1909. See Appendix II for their itinerary. By good fortune Crowley had with him his copy of the Enochian calls. They arrived in Algiers on 17th November; took a train[95] 34 kilometres south to L'Arba (Larbaâ)

---

95. Crowley writes of going by tram (perhaps because the line ran down the centre of the road), but all illustrations depict locomotives.

21. Alexandre Leroux, Alger. *L'Arba – Arrival of the train from Algiers*. Postcard, c.1909.[96]

and started walking in a southerly direction.

After two nights in the open and *"one at a hovel that may have looked so tired on account of its Sisyphean struggle to pretend to be an (sic) hotel,"* [97] they arrived in Aumale (Sour El Ghozlane) on the 21st, where they stayed at the Grand Hotel Grossat. Crowley had no special magical objective in going to Algeria, other than *"renewing the austere rapture of sleeping on the ground and watching the stars, serenely silent above us"*.

However, on 23 November 1909,

"A hand suddenly smote its lightening into my heart and I knew now, that very day, I must take up the 'vision and the voice' from the point I had laid it down nine years ago in Mexico." [98]

After dinner they invoked the Twenty-Eigth Æthyr. The complete record, *The Vision and the Voice (Liber 418)*, is probably his most important work after the *Book of Law*. There is no publically available record of anyone previous to Crowley (including Dee and Kelley) investigating these celestial realms. His pioneering work with the Æthyrs has been an inspiration to many.

Leaving Sour El Ghozlane by the Bou Saâda Gate, they walked to Bou Saâda doing roughly one Æthyr a day, reaching there on the 30th November.

---

96. Leroux (1836-1912) operated several photographic studios in Algiers. Sourced with grateful acknowledgement from *Mémoire des lettres et photos des Jeandet, Gambey, Fumey, Vidal* at www.fumey-jacques.com. 97. *The Confessions*, p.663. 98. *The Confessions*, p.665.

The Twenty-Sixth and Twenty-Fifth Æthyrs were completed at Siddi Aïssa and Aïn El Hadjel and several more were scryed in the vicinity of Bou Saâda, including the infamous Tenth Æthyr with the Demon Choronzon in a nearby lonely valley on 6th December. From there, they headed to Biskra on the 8th December, working the Sixth and Fifth Æthyrs at Ben S'Rour and Tolga. They arrived in fashionable Biskra on the 16th, staying at the Royal Hotel, and finally completing their visionary journey on 19th December with LIL, the First Æthyr. They returned to London on New Year's Eve, 1909.

Crowley's usual method of working is worth detailing:

• *I had with me a great golden topaz (set in a calvary cross of 6 squares, made of wood, painted vermilion) engraved with a greek cross and 5 squares charged with the rose of 49 petals.*

• *I held this as a rule in my hand. After choosing a spot where I was not likely to be disturbed, I would take this stone and recite the Enochian Key, and after satisfying myself that the invoked forces were actually present, made the topaz play a part not unlike the looking-glass in the case of Alice...*

• *I described what I saw and repeated what I heard and Frater O.V.* [99] *[Victor Neuburg – "the Scribe"] would write down my words and any phenomena observed.* [100]

• Various additional features were sometimes added to aid effectiveness, such as having sex with Neuburg within a magic circle built from rocks, while working

22. Dreyluss Freres. *Aumale (Sour El Ghozlane), Bou Saâda Gate (La Porte Sud)*. Postcard, c.1910 (Author's Collection).

---

99. Frater Omnia Vincam (Latin: 'I will conquer all.') 100. *The Confessions*, p. 669.

23. Neurdein Phot. *Biskra - The Royal Hotel.* Postcard, January 1910. Crowley checked out at the end of December 1909. (Author's collection)

the Fourteenth Æthyr on a small mountain (Da'leh Addin) near Bou Saâda on 3rd December.[101] Crowley declared the 14th Æthyr a success which he claimed aided his understanding of the Magister Templi Grade.

The most famous or rather infamous Æthyr working is the manifestation of the demon Choronzon, the Dweller of the Abyss and the personification of disharmony and confusion, in the 10th Æthyr or ZAX in a lonely valley near Bou Saâda (on 6 December). Choronzon ("Coronzom" in Dee's diaries) was described to Edward Kelley by the Angel Gabriel on 21 April 1584 :

> *"Man in his creation... was exalted, and so became holy in the sight of God, until that Coronzom (for so is the true name of that mighty devil) ... Began to assail him ...And so lost [him] the garden of felicity".*[102]

---

101. Da'leh Addin is untraceable today, Crowley's original manuscript offers two alternatives, Djebel Zaab and Daleh Uzdu (see *The Vision and the Voice* (1998), p.139), neither of which are in the vicinity of Bou Saâda, if in fact anywhere. Whereas "djebel" means mountain, "daleh/ da'leh" is not Arabic. However, the searchable GeoNames website (http://www.geonames.org) shows a small mountain or hill Koubet el Fennd (582m.) on the edge of the desert not far away which ticks all the boxes. The record suggests they did not walk miles. 102. *T&FR,* p. 92.

The ceremony took the following form

- Neuburg constructed and purified the stone circle and sat in the centre.
- The demon was summoned into a restraining Triangle outside the circle, where Crowley sat, completely covered by a black robe, invoking the Tenth Æthyr. He went into a deep trance in order to act as medium for any spiritual forces. He had already sacrificed a pigeon at each point of the triangle, and their blood was poured within the triangle to aid manifestation.
- To the hallucinating Neuburg, Choronzon, the Dweller of the Abyss, now occupied the Triangle not Crowley, and seemingly appeared in many forms with many voices mouthing obscenities to Neuburg.
- The demon threw sand onto the Magical Circle, thereby creating a gap through which he immediately rushed. Choronzon/Crowley, pounced, but Neuburg struck him with the Magical Dagger sending him back subdued to The Triangle.

Crowley believed that by astrally identifying and suffering with the demon *"each anguish, each rage, each despair, and each insane outburst"* [103] he could cross the Abyss to a purer state.

For him this initiation was the magical experience of ZAX, the Tenth Æthyr. Others could probably achieve this without the aid of Choronzon, but it would still be hard work all the same. Obviously, only the arch-fiend himself would be good enough for Crowley, who claimed the operation a success. He felt that through his work with the Æthyrs, he had now progressed from not only understanding the grade of Magister Templi or Master of the Temple but to actually achieving it.

Crowley and Victor Neuburg returned to Algeria in December 1910 to start working with the Great Table of the Watchtowers. However, they failed dismally and gave-up. Being caught in torrential downpours for three days, literally dampening their spirits, did not help matters either.

"There was no opening in the furious grey heaven; the wind raged and the rain poured." [104]

It probably would have been better if they had commenced the whole spiritual journey with the Watchtowers, rather than the Æthyrs, as this would have provided an elemental foundation or base from which to explore the Æthyrs; but then, as Crowley himself admitted, when he began exploring the Æthyrs in Mexico with the Thirtieth Key back in 1900, he did not have the necessary experience to make such

103. *The Vision and the Voice* (1998), p. 25   104. *The Confessions*, p. 710.

a choice. For further details of this second Algerian episode, see the Introduction and the Map on page 166.[105] From Bou Saâda they diverted south through desolate desert terrain and across a chain of mountains, arriving in Biskra via the remote, storm-battered township of Ouled Djellal, having decided against a more difficult route through Sidi Khaled. They argued endlessly during the trip and returned home separately, with Crowley leaving Neuburg in Biskra. Having commenced his journey, Crowley was suddenly filled with literary inspiration. He left the train at El Kantara ("The Mouth of the Desert"), just over ninety miles north-east of Biskra, and wrote *The Scorpian: A Tragedy in Three Acts* (1910). Victor Neuburg, on the other hand, felt that Crowley had abandoned him in the desert and later returned home via Tunis.

Crowley continued to be fascinated by Enochian Magic for the rest of his life. Here are some of his last words on the subject. In 1943, he began a correspondence with an unnamed lady giving advice on magical matters, which was published as *Magick without Tears* in 1954. This is from a letter dating from about 1944.

"Before closing the subject entirely I think it well to point out that there are quite a number of worlds on which a good deal of work remains to be done. In particular I cannot refrain from mentioning the work of Dr. Dee and Sir Edward Kelley. My own work on this subject has been so elaborate and extensive that I shall never sufficiently regret that I never had an opportunity of completing it, but I should like to emphasize that the obtaining of a book like *"Liber 418"* [*The Vision and the Voice*] is in itself so outstanding an achievement that it should serve as an encouragement to all magicians".

105. See Crowley's detailed account in *'A Blizzard in the Sahara'*, The Bystander, No.378, Vol. XXIX (March 1, 1911), pages 442 & 444. Also online at www.100thmonkeypress.com (accessed 5.7.2019)

APPENDIX 11

ALEISTER CROWLEY, VICTOR NEUBERG AND THE ÆTHYRS:

THE ITINERY

30	TEX	1900	14th November	Mexico (Crowley only)
29	RII		17th November	Mexico (Crowley only)
28	BAG	1909	23th November	Aumale (Sour el Ghozlane), Algeria.
			8:00-9:00 p.m.	They arrived in Algiers on 17th. Train to L'Arba (Larbaâ). Walked to Aumale, arriving 21st. Stayed at Hotel Grossat. On 24th they left on foot by the Bou Saâda Gate (La Porte Sud) for Bou Saâda.
27	ZAA		24th November 8:00-9:00 p.m.	Sidi Aïssa.
26	DES		25th November 1:10-2:00 p.m.	Desert near Sidi Aïssa
25	VTI		25th November 8:40-9:40 p.m.	Aïn el Hadjel
24	NIA		26th November 2:00-3:25 p.m.	Aïn el Hadjel
23	TOR		28th November 9:30-10:15 p.m.	Bou Saâda
22	LIN		28th November 4:00-6:00 p.m.	Bou Saâda

21	ASP	29th November 1:30-2:50 p.m.	Desert near Bou Saâda
20	CHR	30th November 9:15-10:50 a.m.	Bou Saâda
19	POP	30th November 10:00-11:45 p.m.	Bou Saâda
18	ZEN	1st December 2:30-4:10 p.m.	Bou Saâda
17	TAN	2nd December 12:15-2:00 a.m.	Bou Saâda
16	LEA	2nd December 4:50-6:05 p.m.	Bou Saâda
15	OXO	3th December 9:15-11:10 a.m.	Bou Saâda

24. Dreyluss Freres. *General view of Bou Saâda*. Postcard, c. 1920
(Author's collection)

14	VTA	3th December (1) 2:50-3:15 p.m. (2) 9:50-11:15 p.m.	Bou Saâda, began on top of nearby Mount Da'leh Addin, performing an act with Victor Neuberg "not lawful to speak of". Completed at Bou Saâda.
13	ZIM	4th December 2:10-3:45 p.m.	River bed near Bou Saâda
12	LOE	4-5th December 11:30 p.m.-1:20 a.m.	Bou Saâda
11	ICH	5th December 10:10-11:35 p.m.	Bou Saâda
10	ZAX	6th December 2:00-4:15 p.m.	Lonely valley of fine sand in the desert near Bou Saâda. (The Choronzon working)
9	ZIP	7th December 9:30-11:10 p.m.	Bou Saâda
8	ZID	8th December 7:10-9:10 p.m	Desert between Bou Saâda and Biskra.
7	DEO	9th December 8:10-10:00 p.m.	W'ain-t-Aissha (Aïoun Aïcha)
6	MAZ	10th December 7:40-9:40 p.m.	Benishrur (Ben S'Rour).
5	LIT	12th December 7:00-8:12 p.m.	Began working in the desert between Ben S'Rour and Tolga. Ceased on the order of an Angel.

		13th December 8.15 – 10.10 p.m	Completed the working at Tolga
4	PAZ	16th December 9:00-10:30 a.m.	Biskra. Stayed at the Royal Hotel.
3	ZOM	17th December 9:30-11:30 a.m.	Biskra
2	ARN	18th December (1) 9:30-10:05 a.m. (2) 10:15-11:52 a.m. (3) 3:10-4:45 p.m.	Biskra . Continued the working at the nearby thermal baths of Hammam Salahin (Salihine).
		20th December (4) 8:35-9:35 p.m.	Finally completed the working at Biskra, after scrying the First Æthyr on the 19th.
1	LIL	19th December 1:30-3:30 p.m.	Biskra
		New Year's Eve, 1909	Aleister Crowley and Victor Neuberg returned to London

25. Auguste Maure. *Tolga*. Postcard, before 1907. (Author's Collection)

26. Nuerdein Phot. *Hammam Salihine*. Postcard, c. 1900 (Author's Collection).

A Note on Biskra

It is interesting that Aleister Crowley chose to explore the Æthyrs on a journey to Biskra as opposed to anywhere else. This was no doubt because, at the end of the nineteenth century, the oasis of Biskra had become a world famous exotic tourist location. Its warm winter climate; the therapeutic hot springs of nearby Hammam Salihine; the novelty of desert life; and a new steam train connection from Algiers in 1888 attracted rich European tourists, whose numbers increased dramatically as a result of the rail link. A French style public garden (Le Jardin Landon) had already been created by French aristocrat Albert Landon de Longueville in 1872 and soon a theatre and two new luxury hotels, The Royal and The Palace with a casino, were established. Biskra's fashionable reputation found favour with the art world and the avant garde, attracting painters such as Henri Matisse, Hippolyte Lazerges, and Maurice Bompard. The place and the local Arab boys fascinated the author André Gide, who stayed there in the mid-1890s, and was inspired to write *L'Immoraliste*; while Béla Bartók, the Hungarian composer and ethnomusicologist, visited in 1913 and made 90 recordings of Arabic and local Chaoula (Berber) songs and music. The orientalist photographer Auguste Maure (1840-1907) lived in Biskra from 1855 until his death and founded the first photography studio, Photographie Saharienne, in southern Algeria.

If he did not know already, Crowley probably would have become aware of the charms of the "Monte Carlo of the South", as Biskra became known, during his many Parisian evenings spent in the company of *"a sort of international clique of writers, painters, sculptors, students and their friends"*[106] in an upper room of Le Chat Blanc restaurant at 13 Rue d'Odessa[107] in the artists' quarter of Montparnasse. When visiting Paris, he always stayed at the now long-gone Hotel de Blois at 50 Rue Vavin, off the Boulevard du Montparnasse. He would frequent nearby local cafes, such as Lavenue and La Rotonde and enjoy an early morning citron pressé in Le Dôme.[108]

Two world wars and the Algerian War of Independence (1954-1962) eventually put an end to Biskra's French colonial extravagance. The magnificent Royal Hotel was demolished in 1980.

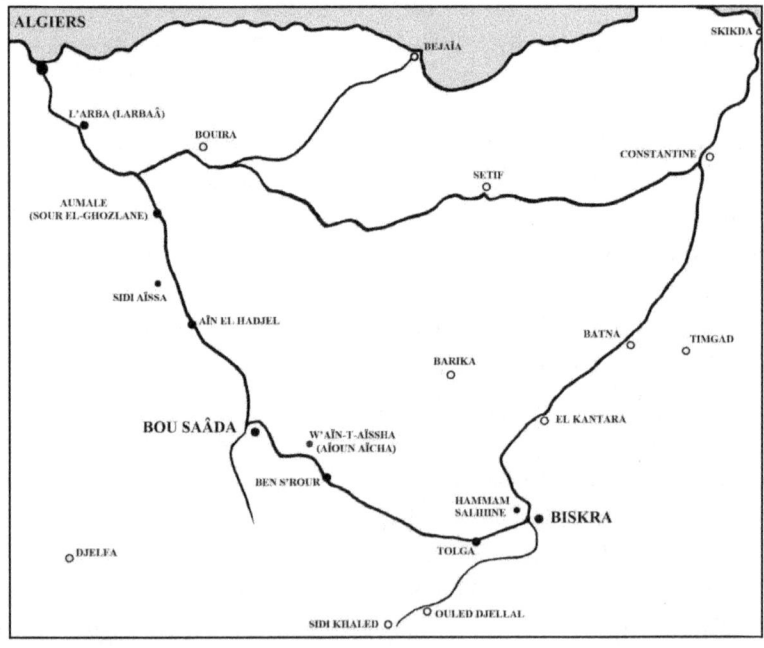

27. Crowley and Neuberg's Algerian Odyssey (© R.E. Cousins)

---

106. *The Confessions*, p.360. 107. The address currently houses a Lebanese restaurant and a French-American diner. With thanks to Nicholas Clements for locating Le Chat Blanc.
108. La Rotonde and Le Dôme are still trading and Lavenue is now the Hippopotamus Grill at 68 Boulevard du Montparnasse. The name, Lavenue, is still visible in stone relief as part of the façade.

APPENDIX III

THE ANGELIC OR ENOCHIAN LANGUAGE

Before midday, on Saturday 26 March 1583, just after a year of his arrival at Dee's house in Mortlake, Edward Kelley received the first form of the Angelic Alphabet. On Monday, 6 May, he received the final perfect form of the letters. Dee noted in his diary,

"That when Edward Kelley could not aptly imitate the forme of the Characters, or letters, as they were shewd: that then they appeared drawn on his paper with a light yelow cullor, which he drew the blak uppon, and so the yelow cullor disappearing: there remayned only the shape of the letter in blak."[109]

Just over a week earlier, a garrulous angel called IL from an angelic order known as the *Sons of the Sons of Light* told them that:

"These letters represent the creation of man: and therefore they must be in proportion. They represent the Workmanship wherewithall the sowle of man was made like unto his Creator." [110]

The Angelical Language has a number of synonyms. It is also known as: Adamical, Angelical, the Celestial Speech, the Divine Language, the Divine Tongue, Enochian (The Golden Dawn termed it so. Dee never referred to it as such), the Holy Language, the Language of Angels, the Language of Enoch, Lingua Adamica, the Speech from God.

Notes

1. It is supposedly the language God used to create the World. Adam spoke with God and named all living things.

Genesis 2:19

And out of the ground the Lord God formed every beast of the field and every fowl of the air; and brought them unto Adam to see what he would call them: and whatsoever Adam called every living creature that was the name thereof.

---

109. Peterson, Joseph, ed. *John Dee's Five Books of Mysteries*, p. 405
110. Ibid, p.373.

CHARACTER	LETTER	NAME
	A	Un
	B	Pa
	C, K	Veh
	D	Gal
	E	Graph
	F	Or
	G, J	Ged
	H	Na
	I, Y	Gon
	L	Ur
	M	Tal
	N	Drux
	O	Med
	P	Mals
	Q	Ger
	R	Don
	S	Fam
	T	Gisg
	U, V	Van
	X	Pal
	Z	Ceph

2. This privilege was lost when Adam was expelled from Paradise (The Fall) together with the loss of the Holy Language.

Ever since, there has been the quest to rediscover the Divine Language and so converse with God and the Angels and thus learn the secrets of Creation and the Universe.

This was particularly so in the Renaissance, where evidence was sought for:

- The possibility of regaining Paradise from a terrestrial existence.
- The existence of the Divine Language.

The Patriarch Enoch provided the proof (especially for Dee and Kelley) that this was possible.

- Enoch, son of Jared and father of Methuselah, was the only person after Adam to achieve this state of exaltation from a terrestrial existence.
- He was the only descendant of Adam privileged to know the Angelic Language which was again lost with The Flood.
- He was the only descendant of Adam not to die:

3. Adam on Earth constructed Proto-Hebrew – the original pure Hebrew – from his memory of Angelical.

4. Enoch was taken by God and learnt the Celestial Speech.

Genesis 5:24

And Enoch walked with God: and he was not: for God took him.

5. He recorded the Celestial Speech for humanity; but the book (Dee's so-called *Book of Enoch* or *Liber Loagaeth* aka *Book of the Speech from God*) was lost in The Flood.

6. Adam's universal language – the Proto Hebrew – split into a thousand tongues after mankind's folly of the Tower of Babel.

7. Modern languages developed, including Biblical Hebrew.

Until Dee and Kelley, only Enoch knew the Lingua Adamica. Various magical alphabets already existed. Both Heinrich Cornelius Agrippa (1485-1535) and Johannes Trithemius (1462-1516) included them in their books.

8. However, as mentioned in Chapter One, it was not the first time for a claim for the discovery of the Language of Enoch. In 1530, the Venetian Priest, Joannes Augustinus Pantheus (Giovanni Agostino Panteo), published the alchemical work,

known as *Vorarchadumia*, which contained an "Alphabet of Enoch". Dee owned a copy that he annotated and which is now in the British Library.

The Book of Enoch – some brief facts

The actual apocryphal *Book of Enoch* (*1 Enoch* or the *Ethiopic Book of Enoch*), with parts dating from about 300 BC, was rediscovered during the eighteenth-century and bears no resemblance to the work delivered to Dee and Kelley supposedly by the angels. Neither does the first-century *Book of the Secrets of Enoch* (*2 Enoch* or the *Slavonic Book of Enoch*) nor *3 Enoch* (the *Hebrew Book of Enoch* or the *Book of Rabbi Ishmael the High Priest*), which dates from about the fifth-century. The content of *3 Enoch* suggests the writer was familiar with *1 Enoch*.

Dee and Kelley's *Liber Loagaeth* contains indecipherable Enochian invocations and 96 tables each consisting of 2,401 alphabetic squares. The book is still as mystifying today as it was to Dee and Kelley back in the sixteenth century.

APPENDIX IV

THE QABALISTICAL INVOCATION OF SOLOMON

Puissances du royaume, soyez sous mon pied gauche et dans ma main droite;
Gloire et Éternité, touchez mes deux épaules et dirigez-moi dans
les voies de la victoire;
Miséricorde et Justice, soyez l'équilibre et la splendeur de ma vie;
Intelligence et Sagasse, donnez-moi la couronne;
Espirits de MALCHUTH, conduisez-moi entre les deux colonnes sur lesquelles
s'appuie tout l'edifice du temple;
Anges de NETSAH et de HOD, affermissez-moi sur la pierre cubique de JESOD;
Ô GÉDULAEL! Ô GÉBURAEL! Ô TIPHERETH!
BINAEL, sois mon amour;
RUACH HOCHMAEL, sois ma lumière;
Sois ce que tu es et ce que tu seras, Ô KETHERIEL!
Ischim, assistez-moi au nom de SADDAÏ.
Cherubim, soyez ma force au nom d'ADONAÏ.
Beni-Elohim, soyez mes frères au nom du fils et par les vertus de ZÉBAOTH.
Eloïm, combattez pou moi au nom de TETRAGRAMMATON.
Malachim, protégez-moi au nom de JOTCHAVAH.
Seraphim, épurez mon amour au nom d'ELVOH.
Hasmalim, éclairez-moi avec les splendeurs d'ELOÏ et de Schechinah.
Aralim, agissez; Ophanim, tournez et resplendissez.
Hajoth a Kadosh, criez, parlez, rugissez, mugissez:
Kadosh, Kadosh, Kadosh
SADDAÏ, ADONAÏ, JOTCHAVAH, EIEAZEREIE.
Hallelu-jah, Hallelu-jah, Hallelu-jah.
Amen Amen

This is original French version of the *Qabalistical Invocation of Solomon* by Éliphas Lévi aka Alphonse Louis Constant (1810-75). It first appeared in his *Rituel de la Haute Magie,* Paris, 1856. The book is the companion volume to *Dogme de la Haute Magie* published the preceding year. Samuel Liddell MacGregor Mathers produced the first English rendering of the invocation, which can be found at the end of his translation of the *Key of Solomon the King* (George Redway, London, 1888). It is quite accurate, but some subtle shades of meaning are occasionally lost. Lévi's two books were later combined in one volume and published by Germer Bailliér Librarie-Editeur as the *Dogme et Rituel de la Haute Magie,* in 1861. Arthur Edward Waite translated this as *Transcendental Magic: its Doctrine and Ritual* (Rider, London, 1896). The book is an acknowledged difficult read, but considering Waite's version of the invocation is suspect in places, this indigestibility may be partly due to his translation.

In February 1896, just before *Transcendental Magic* was published, another version of the invocation appeared. Entitled *The Kabbalistic Prayer*, it featured in the closing pages of *The Magical Ritual of the Sanctum Regnum*[111], a previously unpublished treatise by Lévi on the Tarot Trumps. This is an expanded version of the invocation. Its lines describe in greater detail the ascent through the Four Worlds of the Qabalah to EHEIEH ASHER EHEIEH. It provides a greater understanding of the process, but lacks the intrinsic ritual punch of the shorter version. *The Magical Ritual of the Sanctum Regnum* was edited and translated into English by Wynn Westcott. Lévi had written the original manuscript on pages interleaved with the text of a printed copy of Johannes Trithemius's *De Septem Secundeis* (1508), which had been published in Cologne in 1567. The book was in the private collection of the Christian esotericist, Edward Maitland (1824-97), and Westcott obtained special permission to translate and publish the manuscript. However, as the original French version of *The Magical Ritual of the Sanctum Regnum* was never published and the location of the manuscript is now uncertain, it is impossible to gauge the accuracy of Westcott's translation.

The majority of occultists are familiar with the invocation. It is often employed in rituals during the initial ceremonies. It links the Microcosm with Macrocosmic forces, activating and aligning the sephirothic power centres of the body, so creating

---

111. Éliphas Lévi, *The Magical Ritual of the Sanctum Regnum*, translated and edited by Wynn Wescott (London, 1896) was reprinted in 1970, by Crispin Press in association with Thorsons Publishers Ltd, London. *The Kabbalistic Prayer* was published separately in 2000 by Holmes Publishing Group, Edmonds WA, USA.

a balance of mind, body and spirit. This allows the magician to receive and direct the higher forces required for realising the objective of the ritual.

The invocation is constructed on the scheme of the Sephiroth of the Tree of Life and as such has a long pedigree. For example, in the fifth chapter of the first book of the *Key of Solomon*, there is a long aspirational conjuration based on this format, which is evident in the first few lines.

"O ye Spirits, ye I conjure by the Power, Wisdom, and Virtue of the Spirit of God, by the uncreate Divine Knowledge, by the vast Mercy of God, by the Strength of God, by the Greatness of God, by the Unity of God; and by the Holy Name of God EHEIEH, which is the root, trunk, source, and origin of all other Divine names ..."[112]

There is a guide to formulating such invocations in the *Siphra Dtzenioutha* or *The Book of Concealed Mystery*.[113]

"When a man wishes to utter his prayers rightly before the Lord", his invocations rise upward from him. Understanding emanates from wisdom; "then that fountain floweth forth plentifully, and spreadeth abroad so as to send down the influx from the Highest". Such a man is "held to intertwine the connecting links of all, namely, those connecting links of true and righteous meditation; and all his petitions shall come to pass." [114]

The petition can be constructed in various ways, full details of which can be found in *The Book of Concealed Mystery*. Lévi's invocation appears to be a combination of the following principles:

- The ten sephiroth or numerations
- The "venerable names of the most holy and blessed God".
- The knowledge of "how to ascend from that which is below to that which is above". And also "how to derive the influx from the highest downward".

The invocation rises through the sephiroth of The Tree of Life from Malkuth to Kether and then repeats the process, first with the god names of the ten sephiroth and then with their corresponding Orders of Angels. In theory, at Kether "The Crown",

---

112. *Key of Solomon the King*, translated by S. Liddell MacGregor Mathers (London: Routledge & Kegan Paul, 1981) p. 26.   113. Published in *The Kabbalah Unveiled*, translated by S. Liddell MacGregor Mathers (London: Routledge & Kegan Paul, 1975) pp. 81-90.   114. Ibid, p.87-88.

the highest point, the aspirant will be enlightened by virtue of the proximity of the Divine, whose influence can then, in turn, be channelled "downward" for the benefit of the earth plane.

To conclude, it is only fair to offer the reader a new translation of *The Qabalistical Invocation of Solomon*.

Powers of the Kingdom, be beneath my left foot, and within my right hand.
Glory and Eternity, touch my two shoulders, and guide me in the ways of Victory.
Mercy and Justice, be the Equilibrium and splendour of my life.
Understanding and Wisdom, give me the Crown.
Spirits of MALKUTH, conduct me between the two pillars upon which rests the whole edifice of the Temple.
Angels of NETZACH and of HOD, make me firm upon the Cubical Stone of YESOD.
O GEDULAEL! O GEBURAEL! O TIPHERETH!
BINAEL, be my Love.
RUACH CHOKMAEL, be my Light.
Be that which Thou art, and that which Thou willest to be, O KETHERIEL!
Ishim, assist me in the Name of SHADAI.
Cherubim, be my strength in the Name of ADONAI.
Beni Elohim, be my brothers in the Name of the Son, and by the virtues of TZABAOTH.
Elohim, fight for me in the Name of TETRAGRAMMATON.
Malachim, protect me in the Name of JEHOVAH.
Seraphim, purify my love in the Name of ELOAH.
Chashmalim, enlighten me with the splendours of ELOI and of SHEKINAH.
Aralim, act; Ophanim, revolve and shine.
Chaioth Ha-Kadosh, cry aloud, speak, roar, and bellow:
Kadosh, Kadosh, Kadosh
SHADAI, ADONAI, JEHOVAH, EHEIEH ASHER EHEIEH
Halelu-Jah Halelu-Jah Halelu-Jah.
Amen. Amen.

APPENDIX V

THE LATIN WALL INSCRIPTION IN TADEÁŠ HÁJEK'S STUDY

Imperial Physician Tadeáš Hájek's house was located in Betlémské Náměstí in Prague by the Bethlehem Chapel (Betlémská Kaple).[115] When John Dee stayed at the house between August 1584 and January 1585, he made a transcription of an alchemical wall inscription in the little study that he and Kelley used for the angelic communications. The text was in Latin and a translation can be found in Chapter Five above, but for the interested reader here is Dee's original transcription from his diary in British Library MS Cotton Appendix XLVI, Part 1 (folio 227v.), which is also printed in *A True and Faithful Relation* on page 212.

"... these verses were over the door
*Immortale Decus par gloriaque illi debentur
Cujus ab ingenio est discolor hic paries.*

And of the Philosophers work (on the South-side of the Study) in three lines, uppermost was this written.

Candida si rubeo mulier nupta sit marito:Mox complectuntur,, Complexa concipiuntur. Per se solvuntur, per se quandoque peificiuntur:Vt duo quæ fuerant, unam in corpora fiant: Sunt duæ res primo, Sol cum Luna, tamen in imo, Confice, videbis, fit ab hiis lapis quoque Rebis.[116]

Lunæ potentate, peregit Sol Rebis actu: Sol adit Lunam per medium, rem facit unam. Sol tendit velum, transit per ecliptica Cœlum:Currit ubi Luna recurrit hunc denno sublima.Vt sibi lux detur, in sole quæ retinetu. Nec abiit vere, sed vult ipsi commanere: illustrans certe defunctum corpus aperte: Si Rebis scires, quid esset tu reperires. Hæc ars est cara, brevis, levis atque rara. Ars nostra est Ludus puere, labor mulierum; scitote omnes filii artis hujus, quod nemo potest colligere fructus nostri; Elixiris, nisi per introitum nostri lapidis Elementati, etsi aliam viam quærit, viam nunquam intrabit nec attinget. Rubigo est Opus, quod fit ex solo aure, dum intraverit in suam humiditatem.

"And so it ended."

---

115. The Chapel was founded in 1391; partially demolished in 1786; then rebuilt in the 1950s from old plans. 116. *T&FR* misprints 'Rebis' (the alchemical hermaphrodite) as 'Rebus' here and again a further four lines down.

Further information on the early history of the house and its ownership can be found in Josef Teige's *Základy starého mistopisu Pražského (1437-1620)*, Volume 1. *Staré Město Pražské*, Part 2. (Prague: 1915), pp. 874-81. Teige (1862-1921) was a Czech historian and archivist. For details on the Bethlehem Chapel and the vicinity, see Alois Kubíček, *Betlémská kaple*. (Prague: Státní Nakladatelství Krásné Literatury, Hudby a Umění 1953).

APPENDIX VI

A KELLEY MISCELLANY

The Legend of Kelley's Tower in Prague
Kelley's supposed house in Jánský Vršek (John's Hill) by Prague Castle is known as The House at [the sign of] the Donkey in the Cradle (Dům u Osla v Kolébce). A rather fanciful local legend explains how the name was acquired and follows herewith. It is from a guide to the house that used to be attached to the exterior doors of the building. The house probably dates from the second half of the sixteenth century. Although there is, as yet, no documentary evidence to support the fact, Kelley allegedly bought the place about 1590 only to lose it, when he was imprisoned by the Emperor Rudolf II for refusing to disclose his alchemical secrets.[117] Kelley's imprisonment led to all his properties and possessions being confiscated, ostensibly in order to clear unsettled debts.

The legend that gave this house the name Donkey In The Cradle
In 1590 on Jánský Vršek in the Malá Strana district of Prague was a house that was a home to the famous astrologist Edward Kelley. His failure to deliver a promised "elixir of life" resulted in the punishment of having his ears cut off. Thereafter, he wore his hair long to keep it secret. His living quarters were located in a section of the attic and he could be found nightly in the sanctuary of this tower charting the stars.

During this same time a young mother lived on the ground floor. When on one stormy night her child fell ill, the desperate woman ran out into the courtyard and found a light coming from the tower windows. In her desperation she called: *"Your Excellency, help me, my baby is dying"*. The astrologist leaned out of the window and a sudden wind blew back his hair and exposed his secret to the woman. He shouted down: *"Go away! Your child shall have the head of a donkey!"*

The horror-stricken woman rushed home where she found her child lying in his cradle and indeed the child's head had transformed into that of a donkey.

On Christmas Day, after having stayed home for three days, she hurried to the church of St Thomas[118], which was located at that time just opposite the house.

---

117. Kelley was incarcerated twice: from 1591-3 in Křivoklát Castle, 30 miles north of Prague; and from 1596-7 in Castle Hněvín in Most, North Bohemia, where he met his end.   118. The church is actually a few streets away from the house, but interestingly Kelley's step-daughter, the poetess Elizabeth Jane Weston or 'Westonia' (1581-1612) is buried in the cloisters.

Crying, she looked up to a picture of the Madonna and prayed for mercy. She tearfully returned home and to her own disbelief found the beautiful face of her son smiling up at her from his cradle. The she fell to her knees gratefully accepting this miracle.

The news spread like wildfire throughout Malá Strana and from that time this house has been known as At the Donkey in the Cradle (U osla v kolébce).

• In truth, the name derives from an old fresco that was on the house depicting The Nativity. Over time, the picture gradually faded away until only the donkey and cradle were discernible, thus giving the house its name. [119] However, this account created a slightly different, alternative name for the house, viz. Dům u Osel u kolébky (The House at the Donkey by the Cradle), by which it is sometimes referred.

Kelley's Ears

On the subject of Kelley's ears, there is little proof that he was in fact earless. The main reference is in John Weever's *Ancient Funerall Monuments* (1631), which provides the original account of Kelley's necromancy in Walton-le-Dale near Preston (see below). The legend is that he wore a skullcap to disguise his lack of ears, but there is no contemporary record of this. According to Dee, during a fracas in Prague with Alexander, a Polish servant, Kelley threw a stone at him and was out in the street "in just doublet & hose without cap or hat on head" [120]. Kelley was hardly hiding his disability in this case.

The cropping of ears - one or both, ear boring, slitting a nostril, branding one side of face, and the pillory were common corporal punishments for fraudulent beggars.

Kelley's supposed punishment (but there is no actual evidence of a crime) apparently resulted from forging wills for which he was supposedly pilloried in Lancaster in 1580 and, consequently, lost both his ears. This was reported by Weever. Other stories have him forging title deeds, when working as a notary in London or coining money. It would have been a terrible stigma for him to have been branded as a criminal, making his later acceptance at the court of the Emperor Rudolf extremely unlikely. However, on 20 July 1593, the diplomat and MP, Christopher Parkins (c.1547 – 1622) wrote to Sir Robert Cecil, second son

---

119. Ruth, F. *Kronika královské Prahy a obcí sousedních, I.* (Praha: 1903) p.369.
120. This incident occurred on 3 September 1584. *T&FR*, p. 229.

of Lord Burghley, from Prague, informing him that one of Rudolf's councillors had asked for "any account of the diminishing of one of his [Kelley's] ears, or of his good or evil behaviour in England" [121] for the benefit of a concerned Emperor. No details of the answer survive.

Kelley At Walton-Le-Dale, Lancashire [122]

The parish church of St. Leonard, Walton-le-Dale, is situated on a ridge overlooking the confluence of the Rivers Darwen and Ribble, just south of Preston. Until the nineteenth century the church was known locally as "Lawe (or Lowe) Chapel". The name derives from the Saxon word "Law" meaning "on an elevation" and may indicate that a wooden church dating from those times originally stood on the site. It is not known when a stone church was first built at Walton. The oldest parts of the present church – the tower and the chancel – date from the first half of the sixteenth century, but an old charter of 1162 indicates a church was already in existence at the time.

The churchyard with tottering gravestones slopes sharply downwards to the steep banks of the River Ribble. It was here in a neighbouring wood, possibly about 1580, that Edward Kelley and a local man, Paul Waring of nearby Dove Cotes, Clayton Brook, allegedly engaged in an act of necromancy and evoked an evil spirit in order to know the future and the circumstances of the death of a "noble young Gentleman" in Waring's charge.

The dark ceremony is described by the antiquary John Weever (1576-1632) in *Ancient Funerall Monuments* (London, 1631). A native of Preston, Weever was told of the event by a servant of the "young Gentleman", who had also assisted Kelley and Waring in that "dismall and abhorrid business". Various "diuers gentlemen and others now liuing in Lancashire", to whom the servant had related the story, confirmed the tale, as did also the noble "Gentleman himselfe a little before his death". The Gentleman informed Weever that he had heard of the conjuration by Kelley "from his said Seruant and Tenant; onely some circumstances excepted; which he thought not fitting to come to his masters knowledge".

Weever recounts the tale as follows: [123]

"This diabolicall questioning of the dead, for the knowledge of future accidents, was put in practise by the foresaid Kelley; who, vpon a certaine night, in the park

---

121. As quoted by Michael Wilding, 'Edward Kelley: A Life', *Cauda Pavonis*, New Series Vol. 18, Nos. 1 & 2, Spring & Fall, 1999. 122. An earlier version of this article appeared in *Talking Stick Magickal Journal*, Issue 1, Vol. II, 1998. 123. *Ancient Funerall Monuments*, pp. 45-46. The original spelling and punctuation has been retained throughout

of Walton in le dale, in the county of Lancaster, with one Paul Waring (his fellow companion in such deeds of darknesse) inuocated some one of the infernall regiment, to know certaine passages in the life, as also what might bee knowne by the deuils foresight, of the manner and time of death of a noble young Gentleman, as then in his wardship. The blacke ceremonies of that night being ended, Kelley demanded of one of the Gentleman's seruants, what corse was last buried in Law-church-yard, a church thereunto adijoyning, who told him of a poore man that was buried there but the same day. Hee and the said Waring intreated this foresaid seruant, to go with them to the graue of the man so lately interred, which hee did; and withall did helpe them to digge up the carcase of the poore caitiffe, whom by their incantations, they made (or rather some euill spirit through his Organs) to speake, who diliuered strange predictions concerning the said Gentleman."

Ultimately, Kelley never prospered from his nefarious pursuits. He allegedly committed suicide with poison on 1 November 1597 after seriously injuring himself, when trying to escape from Castle Hněvín in Most, where he had been imprisoned by the Emperor Rudolf II for failing to disclose his alchemical secrets and produce gold. It was left to his step-daughter Elizabeth Jane Weston (1581-1612), the Latin poetess "Westonia" and a favourite of both the Emperor and Prague Humanist Circles, to restore the family's reputation and regain the possessions confiscated upon Kelley's incarceration. Could this early act of necromancy at Walton-le-Dale be the cause of all Kelley's subsequent misfortunes? For as Weever says:

"These iniuries done against the dead, who ought to sleepe in peace untill the last sound of the Trumpet, haue euer beene, euen amongst the very Pagans themselues, esteemed execrable. Insomuch that if any man who was knowne to have committed such a hainous offence, and did by chance escape the hand of humane Iustice, yet he could not (in their opinion), avoid the punishment of the diuine powers."

28. St Leonard's Church, Walton-le-Dale (Photograph © R.E. Cousins)

APPENDIX VII

FORM FOR RECORDING RESULTS

By completing this form, a picture of the Enochian worlds visited can be created by combining the results of all participants. Any category not covered can be included in "Any Other Information" at the end of each section. Please do not provide interpretations of events seen, nor reveal any personal information or emotions generated by the ritual. Non-one will be identified. If completed and returned by email attachment, they can be printed out and shuffled before analysing in order to maintain anonymity.

Eastern Quarter
AIR OF EAST

1. **Extra-Terrestrial**

Cosmic imagery

Forces

2. **Terrestrial**

Airspace

Seascape

Landscape

Season

Day or Night

Weather

3. Terrestrial Features

Terrain

Vegetation

Buildings

Transport

---

4. Life Forms

Angelic

Animal/ Marine etc.

Human

Non-Human

---

5. Other Senses

Sounds

Smell

Touch (e.g. texture of objects)

---

6. General Mood (Optional)
E.g. Did visions create general feeling of peace, irritation etc.

---

7. Any other Information

This basic format of these seven categories can be repeated for the Water, Earth and Fire aspects of the Eastern Quarter. It is omitted here for reasons of space. Continue using this format for recording the results of pathworkings for the elements of the Southern, Western, and Northern Quarters. Visionary journeys in the Aires or Æthyrs should be recorded in the same fashion. A template for the Aires follows.

The Aires
Record number of Aire / Æthyr and Name, e.g. 30 TEX

1. Extra-Terrestrial
Cosmic imagery

Forces

---

2. Terrestrial
Airspace

Seascape

Landscape

Season

Day or Night

Weather

---

3. Terrestrial Features
Terrain

Vegetation

Buildings

Transport

---

4. Life Forms
Angelic

Animal/ Marine etc.

Human

Non-Human

5. Other Senses

Sounds

Smell

Touch (e.g. texture of objects)

---

6. General Mood (Optional)
E.g. Did visions create general feeling of peace, irritation etc.

---

7. Any other Information

SELECT BIBLIOGRAPHY

AGRIPPA VON NETTESHEIM, Heinrich Cornelius. *Three Books of Occult Philosophy*, ed. Donald Tyson. Woodbury, Minnesota: Llewellyn Publications, 1993.

BENJAMIN, Roger. *Biskra: sortilèges d'une oasis*. Paris: Institut du Monde Arabe, 2016.

COUSINS, Robin E. "An appointment with Choronzon?" in *Talking Stick Magickal Journal*, Issue 1, Vol. II. London, 1998, pp. 127-141.

COUSINS, Robin E. *Dr Dee and the Dark Venus: the enigma of the Tuba Veneris*. 2nd ed. London: Neptune Press, 2013.

COUSINS, Robin E. "The geographical location of the Ninety-one Parts of the Earth". Revised ed., in Lon Milo Duquette, *Enochian Vision Magick*, San Francisco: Weiser Books, 2008, pp. 212-223.

CROWLEY, Aleister. *777 and other Qabalistic Writings of Aleister Crowley*, ed. Israel Regardie. Revised edition. Boston, MA: Red Wheel / Weiser, 1987.

CROWLEY, Aleister and Lon Milo DuQuette. *Enochian World of Aleister Crowley: Enochian Sex Magick*. Scottsdale, Arizona: New Falcon Publications, 1991.

CROWLEY, Aleister. *Liber Chanokh Sub Figurâ LXXXIV: A Brief Abstract of the Symbolic Representation of the Universe derived by Dr John Dee through the scrying of Edward Kelly*. Sequim, WA: Holmes Publishing Group, 2001.

CROWLEY, Aleister. *The Vision and the Voice*, edited with an introduction by Israel Regardie. Dallas, Texas: Sangreal Foundation, Inc., 1972.

CROWLEY, Aleister with Victor B. Neuberg and Mary Desti. *The Vision and the Voice* with commentary and other papers. York Beach, ME: Samuel Weiser Inc., 1998. (*The Equinox*, Volume IV, No.II). New edition with extensive commentary by Crowley and new material from manuscript notebooks.

DEE, John. *John Dee's Five Books of Mystery*, ed. by Joseph Peterson. San Francisco: Weiser, 2003.

DEE, John. *Diary for the years 1595-1601*, ed. by John E. Bailey. 1880. Reprinted Kessinger 2010.

DEE, John. *Private Diary of Dr John Dee*, ed. by James Orchard Halliwell. London: Camden Society, 1842. Reprinted Kessinger 1998, Dodo Press 2009; Biblio Bazaar 2009.

DEE, John. *A True and Faithful Relation of what passed for many years between Dr John Dee and some Spirits*, ed. by Meric Casaubon. London, 1659. Reprinted with introduction by Lon Milo DuQuette, New York: Magickal Childe Publishing, 1992. Kessinger paperback edition, 1999. Apocryphile Press edition, 2007

DR RUDD'S NINE HIERARCHIES OF ANGELS, transcribed by Frederick Hockley, edited with an Introduction by Alan Thorogood. York Beach,ME: The Teitan Press, 2013.

DuQUETTE, Lon Milo. *Enochian Vision Magick: An Introduction and Practical Guide to the Magick of Dr. John Dee and Edward Kelley*. San Francisco: Weiser Books, 2008.

FENTON, Edward (ed.). *Diaries of John Dee*. Charlbury, Oxfordshire: Day Books, 1998.

FULLER, Jean Overton. *The Magical Dilemma of Victor Neuberg: A Biography*. Revised ed. Oxford: Mandrake, 2005.

HIPPOCRATES JUNIOR (Pseud.). *The Predicted Plague*. London: Simpkin, Marshall, Hamilton, Kent Co., 1900.

BIBLIOGRAPHY

HONORIUS OF THEBES and Joseph Peterson. *The Sworn Book of Honorius - Liber Iuratus Honorii.* Lake Worth FL: Ibis Press, 2016.

JAMES, Geoffrey. *Enochian Evocation of Dr John Dee.* San Francisco: Red Wheel / Weiser, 2009.

KING, Francis, and Stephen Skinner. *Techniques of High Magic: a Manual of Self-Initiation.* London: C.W. Daniel Co Ltd [1976].

KNIGHT, Gareth. *A Practical Guide to Qabalistic Symbolism.* Cheltenham, Glos: Helios, 1972. 2 vols.

LAYCOCK, Donald C. *Complete Enochian Dictionary.* York Beach, ME: Weiser, 2001.

LEITCH, Aaron. *The Angelical Language.* Woodbury, Minnesota: Llewellyn Publications, 2010. 2 volumes.

LEITCH, Aaron. *The essential Enochian grimoire.* Woodbury, Minnesota: Llewellyn Publications, 2014.

MATHERS, S. Liddell Mac Gregor (ed.). *The Key of Solomon the King* (Clavicula Salomonis). London: Routledge & Kegan Paul, 1888 (1981).

OWEN, Alex. *The Place of Enchantment: British Occultism and the Culture of the Modern.* Chicago: University of Chicago Press, 2004.

SHOEMAKER, David. *The Winds of Wisdom.* Sacramento, California: Anima Solis Books, 2017. First published by Nephilim Press, 2016.

SKINNER, Stephen. *The Complete Magician's Tables.* Singapore: Golden Hoard Press, 2006.

SKINNER , Stephen and David Rankine(eds). *Practical Angel Magick of Dr John Dee's Enochian Tables.* London: Golden Hoard Press, 2004.

SUSTER, Gerald (ed.) *John Dee.* Berkley,CA: North Atlantic Books, 2003. (Western Esoteric Master Series). Reprint of *John Dee: essential readings.* Aquarian Press, 1986.

SZONYI, György. *John Dee's Occultism – Magical exaltation through Powerful Signs.* State University of New York Press, 2004 (2010). Academic study of the Renaissance quest for the Divine in relation to Dee's work.

TURBA PHILISOPHORUM or *Assembly of Philosophers.* [possibly 12th century] Available online at the Alchemy Web Site http://www.levity.com/alchemy/turba.html (accessed 2nd September 2018).

TURNER, Robert. *Elizabethan Magic.* Element Books, 1989. Out of Print. Includes Angelic manuscripts from British Library Sloane MS 3191 with Great Table invocations.

TYSON, Donald. *Enochian Magick for Beginners.* St Paul: Minnesota: Llewellyn, 1997.

VLČEK, Pavel and Kolektiv. *Umělecké památky Prahy: Malá Strana.* Prague: Akademia, 1999.

WOOLLEY, Benjamin. *The Queen's Conjurer – the science and magic of Dr Dee.* London: Harper Collins, 2001.

ZALEWSKI, Pat. *Golden Dawn Enochian Magic.* St Paul: Minnesota: Llewellyn, 1990.

OTHER TITLES BY THOTH PUBLICATIONS

SECRETS OF A GOLDEN DAWN TEMPLE
by Chic Cicero and Sandra Tabatha Cicero

A Hands on Manual for Building a Complete Golden Dawn Temple and Understanding its Symbolism.

The act of constructing a wand or other ritual object is an act of magic. The magician spends an extraordinary amount of time creating ritual objects, not because it is only through these objects that magic can rightly be performed, but because the act of creating is a magical process of growth, one which initiates the development of the will in accordance with the divine intent or purpose. This in turn contributes to the success of the ritual.

The construction of a ritual object should be treated like any othermagical operation. It should focus all parts of the magician's mind (intellect, creativity, imagination, spiritual self) into one purpose – to manifest an object which will be a receptacle for higher forces, in order that the magician too can become a worthy receptacle of that which is divine.

It is not necessary to create a perfect work of art. A person who works long and hard on a wand that looks crude will ultimately have more success than a person who purchases a ready-made wand that is flawless. With this book, clear instructions are finally available on how to fabricate the wands and implements of the Golden Dawn, some of the most significant, profound and beautiful of all the ritual tools that have ever been produced in the Western Magical Tradition.

The various tools presented here each have a very specific symbology attached to them. With the materials and tools available to the modern magician, these instruments can be recreated with stunning accuracy and magnificence.

Chic Cicero and S.Tabatha Cicero have been instrumental in preserving the mystical wisdom of the Hermetic Order of the Golden Dawn. Their *Secrets of a Golden Dawn Temple: The Alchemy and Crafting of Magickal Implements* was the first book to bring you detailed instructions on crafting and using the ritual implements of the Golden Dawn system of magic. Now their classic text has been updated.

This is the most complete book to date on the construction of the many tools used in the Golden Dawn system of magic. Here is a unique compilation of the various tools of the Golden Dawn, all described in full: wands, swords, elemental tools, Enochian Tablets, altars, temple furniture, banners, pillars, thrones, lamens, mantles and robes, ritual headdresses and ceremonial clothing, admission badges, and much more. This book provides complete step-by-step instructions for the construction of nearly 80 different implements, all displayed in photographs or drawings, along with the exact symbolism behind each and every item.

ISBN 978-1-870450-64-5 400 pages

PRINCIPLES OF HERMETIC PHILOSOPHY
Dion Fortune & Gareth Knight

Principles of Hermetic Philosophy was the last known work written by Dion Fortune. It appeared in her Monthly letters to members and associates of the Society of the Inner Light between November 1942 and March 1944.

Her intention in this work is summed up in her own words: "The observations in these pages are an attempt to gather together the fragments of a forgotten wisdom and explain and expand them in the light of personal observation."

She was uniquely equipped to make highly significant personal observations in these matters as one of the leading practical occultists of her time. What is more, in these later works she feels less constrained by traditions of occult secrecy and takes an altogether more practical approach than in her earlier, well known textbooks.

Gareth Knight takes the opportunity to amplify her explanations and practical exercises with a series of full page illustrations, and provides a commentary on her work

ISBN 978-1-870450-34-8

THE STORY OF DION FORTUNE
As told to Charles Fielding and Carr Collins.

Dion Fortune and Aleister Crowley stand as the twentieth century's most influential leaders of the Western Esoteric Tradition. They were very different in their backgrounds, scholarship and style.

But, for many, Dion Fortune is the chosen exemplar of the Tradition – This book tells of her formative years and of her development.

At the end, she remains a complex and enigmatic figure, who can only be understood in the light of the system she evolved and worked to great effect.

There can be no definitive "Story of Dion Fortune". If incomplete, this retrospect provides an insight which provides understanding of her service to her times and ours. Readers may find themselves led into an experience of initiation as envisaged by this fearless and dedicated woman.

ISBN 978-1-870450-33-1

THE CIRCUIT OF FORCE
by Dion Fortune.
With commentaries by Gareth Knight.

In "The Circuit of Force", Dion Fortune describes techniques for raising the personal magnetic forces within the human aura and their control and direction in magic and in life, which she regards as 'the Lost Secrets of the Western Esoteric Tradition'.

To recover these secrets she turns to three sources.
a) the Eastern Tradition of Hatha Yoga and Tantra and their teaching on raising the "sleeping serpent power" or kundalini;

b) the circle working by means of which spiritualist seances concentrate power for the manifestation of some of their results;

c) the linking up of cosmic and earth energies by means of the structured symbol patterns of the Qabalistic Tree of Life.

Originally produced for the instruction of members of her group, this is the first time that this material has been published for the general public in volume form. Gareth Knight provides subject commentaries on various aspects of the etheric vehicle, filling in some of the practical details and implications that she left unsaid in the more secretive esoteric climate of the times in which she wrote.

Some quotes from Dion Fortune's text:

"When, in order to concentrate exclusively on God, we cut ourselves off from nature, we destroy our own roots. There must be in us a circuit between heaven and earth, not a one-way flow, draining us of all vitality. It is not enough that we draw up the Kundalini from the base of the spine; we must also draw down the divine light through the Thousand-Petalled Lotus. Equally, it is not enough for our mental health and spiritual development that we draw down the Divine Light, we must also draw up the earth forces. Only too often mental health is sacrificed to spiritual development through ignorance of, or denial of, this fact."

"....the clue to all these Mysteries is to be sought in the Tree of Life. Understand the significance of the Tree; arrange the symbols you are working with in the correct manner upon it, and all is clear and you can work out your sum. Equate the Danda with the Central Pillar, and the Lotuses with the Sephiroth and the bi-sections of the Paths thereon, and you have the necessary bilingual dictionary at your disposal – if you known how to use it."

ISBN 978-1-870450-28-7

THE WESTERN MYSTERY TRADITION
Christine Hartley

A reissue of a classic work, by a pupil of Dion Fortune, on the mythical and historical roots of Western occultism. Christine Hartley's aim was to demonstrate that we in the West, far from being dependent upon Eastern esoteric teachings, possess a rich and potent mystery tradition of our own, evoked and defined in myth, legend, folklore and song, and embodied in the legacy of Druidic culture.

More importantly, she provides practical guidelines for modern students of the ancient mysteries, 'The Western Mystery Tradition,' in Christine Hartley's view, 'is the basis of the Western religious feeling, the foundation of our spiritual life, the matrix of our religious formulae, whether we are aware of it or not. To it we owe the life and force of our spiritual life.'

ISBN 978 1 870450 24 9

A MODERN MAGICIAN'S HANDBOOK
Marian Green

This book presents the ancient arts of magic, ritual and practical occult arts as used by modern ceremonial magicians and witches in a way that everyone can master, bringing them into the Age of Aquarius. Drawing on over three decades of practical experience, Marian Green offers a simple approach to the various skills and techniques that are needed to turn an interest into a working knowledge of magic.

Each section offers explanations, guidance and practical exercises in meditation, inner journeying, preparation for ritual, the arts of divination and many more of today's esoteric practices. No student is too young or too old to benefit from the material set out for them in this book, and its simple language may help even experienced magicians and witches understand their arts in greater depth.

ISBN 978-1-870450-43-0

www.ingramcontent.com/pod-product-compliance
Lightning Source LLC
Chambersburg PA
CBHW031628160426
43196CB00006B/331